INTERNATIONALS

WHO LIVE

AMONG US

DOING WORLD MISSIONS AT HOME

INTERNATIONALS
WHO LIVE
AMONG US
DOING WORLD MISSIONS AT HOME

NEAL PIROLO

Emmaus Road International

Also by Neal Pirolo
  Serving As Senders
  Serving As Senders~Today
  The Reentry Team
  I Think God Wants Me to be a Missionary

By Neal & Yvonne Pirolo
  Prepare For Battle

First printing, July 2013

Some Scripture quotations are paraphrases of the author.
The masculine pronoun is used throughout without bias.

Cover design by Patty Rappa; www.pattyrappa.com
Cover photos by Ed Compean and iStockphoto
Text formatted by Julie Corrigan; www.thouartinspired.com

Published and Distributed by Emmaus Road International, Inc.
7150 Tanner Court, San Diego, CA 92111 USA
Emmaus_Road@eri.org
www.eri.org

Printed in the United States of America
ISBN 978-1-880185-08-7

"It shall be that you will divide (the land) by lot
as an inheritance for yourselves
and for the strangers who dwell among you.
They shall be to you as native-born...
they shall have an inheritance with you...."
Ezekiel 47:22

To the hundreds of thousands of internationals
who are living among us
and to the thousands who are sharing
the Love of Christ with them.

ACKNOWLEDGEMENTS

"Now unto Him
Who is able to do exceeding abundantly,
above all that we can ask or think;
unto Him be glory throughout all ages."
Ephesians 3:20

First, and foremost, we acknowledge our dependence on God, the Holy Spirit, Who is our inspiration.

My wife, Yvonne, has been my faithful companion for 56 years. Her encouragement and clear suggestions have formed this writing into a valuable resource for *world missions at home*. Thanks!

Our assistant, Julie, has read and reread the manuscript, making notable suggestions. Thanks!

Three families of friends, John and Susan, Jerry and Shellie, and Ed and Susan provided excellent critiquing. I had asked for a "tough" edit. They gave it! Thanks!

Don had a particular interest in Chapter Three: Missionary Kids: Citizens of the World. At one point he apologized for all of the phrases and sentences he had highlighted in yellow. I responded that his yellow was like gold to me. Thanks!

Victor, Robby, Jim and Rose added their help. Thanks!

Our Praise & Prayer Support Team deserve a great Thank You for their faithfulness, especially during those urgent SOS calls to prayer when things were going particularly hard. Thanks!

And a hearty Thank You to a most generous couple who provided the funds for the first print run. Thanks!

TABLE OF CONTENTS

The Field is the WORLD! This has been a battle cry for cross-cultural outreach ministry ever since Jesus explained His parable of the Sower and the Seed to His disciples. (See Matthew 13:38.) The field is the world. As each Christian society has taken up the banner of world evangelization, they have lifted their eyes to the lost in nations _other_ than their own. Notably, in recent history,

-the bold moves of William Carey to the shores of India,

-the daring advances of Hudson Taylor to the interior of China,

-the challenging steps of Cameron Townsend into the jungles of tribal people, and

-the searching spotlight for the unreached peoples of the 10/40 Window by Luis Bush were initiatives of gigantic proportion to reach the lost of the world.

There will be millions around the Throne worshipping the Eternal God of the Universe because of their foresight and their obedience to God. I would call this **Distant Cross-Cultural Outreach.**

"The field is the _world_," Jesus said. In the 21st Century, another initiative has been launched. Let's call it **Local Cross-Cultural Outreach.** The Internet is abuzz with talk about the Diaspora, the millions of souls scattered throughout the world—forcibly or willingly. The word Diaspora means "people on the move," such as Iraqis are in Toronto, Filipinos are in Jerusalem, and East Indians are in the Philippines. Bringing it closer to home, it means Somalis are in Indianapolis, Mexicans are in Seattle, Chinese are in New York City, Arabs are in Dearborn, Vietnamese are in San Diego, and the peoples of the world are in every city and town in America.

Some organizations have been focused on certain groups of internationals, even for decades, such as International Students Incorporated. Several in more recent times, such as Lausanne's Mission America Coalition, are taking bold steps into this expansive, unreached field: *Internationals Who Live Among Us!*

However, engaging the local church to minister Christ's love to internationals in a culturally appropriate manner is coming at a slower pace. But many are awakening to the realization that God has brought the internationals of the world to the doorstep of every church in America!

Oh, they came in previous generations, but they came and "melted into the pot" called America. Today, they are coming in even greater numbers, but they are not becoming *American*. They are maintaining their language, their foods, their culture, their religion; they are not pledging "allegiance to the flag of the United States of America." They are changing the face of America. Demographers are calling it a pluralistic society. "We are no longer just a Christian nation," said a U.S. president.

Don't get me wrong. I fly the American flag on my front porch, and not just on the Fourth of July. I vote in every election. I obey the laws of the "land of the free; the home of the brave." I am grieved when I look over my grandchildren's eighth grade United States civics book and see a whole chapter favorably speaking of another culture's religion and giving only a few pages to the religious beliefs of the founders of America—and those, spoken of in a negative tone. I love the America in which I was raised.

Now, we could get political about this changing face of America, raise any number of banners of objection and determine to correct this phenomenon. Or, we could take our rightful place, seated together with Christ in the heavenlies (See Ephesians 2:6.) and recognize that in this world there are really only two kingdoms: The Kingdom of God and the kingdom of darkness. All seven-plus billion of us are subjects of one or the other.

Paul the Apostle was raised as a Roman citizen. Rome ruled the known world. Caesar was "god!" Yet, within that society Paul chose to declare his position, following the commandment that he had heard on the road to Damascus, when Jesus said: *"...I now send you (to the Gentiles) to open their eyes in order to turn them from darkness to light, and from the power of satan to God, that they might receive forgiveness of sins and an inheritance among those who are sanctified by faith in Me."* Paul continued, *Therefore, King Agrippa, I could not be disobedient to the heavenly vision* (Acts 26:18-19).

And, today, with the increasing number of internationals coming to live among us, we have the choice—it should be our mandate—to follow in the footsteps of Jesus to *"seek and to save the lost"* (Luke 19:10).

Yes, we will have to bridge some cultural differences to be accepted by them.

Yes, we will have to learn to communicate in terms understandable to them in order to present the Gospel and teachings of Christ in a context that is relevant to them.

Yes, we will have to learn to sit on the floor as we eat their foods—with our fingers! Or, at a low table with chopsticks.

Yes, we will have to learn enough of their language to be courteous.

xii INTERNATIONALS WHO LIVE AMONG US

Yes, below the surface of what we can see and hear, we will have to learn to understand their feelings and attitudes and world perspectives.

Yes, we will have to study their religion and culture so we can find the redemptive analogy—that bridge to understanding, for God has placed *"eternity in their hearts"* (Ecclesiastes 3:11).

Yes, local cross-cultural outreach will involve learning new things and possibly doing things in new ways. The difference is that God has brought these internationals of the world to live among us.

In large cities, they number in the thousands, even hundreds of thousands. Yet, within twenty miles of every community in America resides an international (*alien*: KJV) who is trying to make sense out of our strange ways, or the circumstances that got him here, or what life will be like *after* he leaves the United States as a result of having been here.

Yes, we will have to take God's Word seriously: *"Do not take advantage of aliens in your land; do them no wrong. They must be treated like any other citizen; love them as yourself..."* (Leviticus 19:33-34).

Jesus said, *"I was a stranger and you took Me in..."* (Matthew 25:35). Let's do likewise.

Ministering by His grace,
Neal Pirolo
San Diego, California

Il mio nome è Cunio Pirolo.

The S.S. Prinz Adalbert was built in 1902. She was in the service of the West Indies route for the Hamburg American Line. Her ill-fated demise was on September 6, 1917. She had been forced into service by England in the Great War, and was torpedoed by a German submarine. However, twelve years before, on March 21, 1905, she sailed out of Naples, Italy, bound for America. For three thousand miles of open seas, being carried as stowage in the hold, hundreds sat huddled against the tempest of the elements. Their silent eyes were hiding fears and uncertainties, hopes and ambitions.

On a cold and foggy April 7th of that year, the S.S. Prinz Adalbert passed under the watchful eyes of the Statue of Liberty, that bronze lady marking the friendship from the people of France to the people of the United States. If any on board could read English, they would have seen the now famous words:

Give me your tired, your poor,
your huddled masses yearning to breathe free.

I recently acquired a copy of that ship's March 21st manifest. On the passenger list was a very important name to me: Cunio Pirolo, my grandfather. He and his wife, Rosina, had lived in the city of Acerra, one of the most ancient cities in Italy. In 332 BC, it was the first Roman city to have people granted the status of Roman citizenship, yet without voting privilege.

Now, 2237 years later, a young man with his wife and oldest son (my father had not yet been born) was shuttled from that steamship dock on the Hudson River Pier by ferryboat to be processed on Ellis Island. Before he stepped off that boat (as tradition would have it), he shouted his name: **Cunio Pirolo**. He was 31. The manifest confirmed that he was not a polygamist, nor an anarchist. He was not crippled or deformed. He was in good physical and mental condition. He was a farm laborer. He could read and write Italian. He had twenty-one U.S. dollars. His final destination was Chicago, Illinois, to visit his cousin, Francisco.

Yet, they were only three of thousands who would be processed that day in a building that had been used as a recruiting station in the Civil War. On the first day of its operation as an immigration center in 1900, 2,251 people were inspected. In 1905, the year my grandfather came, 1,026,499 immigrants were welcomed to the shores of the "land of the free; the home of the brave."

B. Colin Hamblin wrote in his *Ellis Island,* Souvenir Guide:

> When the great steamships of the early 20th century sailed into New York Harbor, the faces of a thousand nations were on board. There were Russian Jews, Irish farmers, Greeks in kilts and slippers, Italians with sharp moustaches, Cossacks with fierce swords, Englishmen in short knickers, and Arabs in long robes. The old world lay behind them.
>
> Ahead was a new life. Gone were the monarchies and kings, the systems of caste and peasantry, of famine and poverty. But also left behind were friends and family, as well as tradition and customs generations old.[1,2]

In those previous generations, they came. They may have had less understanding of all that they would face here. They probably had fewer connections with others who had come before. But they came expecting to stay and to create a new life. They became Americans. They learned English, or at least their children did. And their children's children definitely were not allowed to learn the language of the *old country*. They proudly waved the "Stars & Stripes." Ambition and hard work in a rapidly growing industrialized country won for them the freedom and satisfaction they sought. America was a melting pot. Traditions and memories of their past died hard, but the refined amalgamation was strong, durable, creative—American. It happened "from sea to shining sea." Therefore Americans, until recent generations, have lived in comparative cultural isolation.

Not possible today! Yes, they are still coming, and in larger numbers than ever before. But they are *not* melting into the pot! They are maintaining their cultural distinctives. International markets allow them to eat their own foods. Major medical centers are staffed to service patients in 28 languages. Even neighborhood "free" clinics can accommodate four or five languages. Housing laws are "winked" at to allow three or four families to live in a single-family dwelling until they can afford their own place. Instructions on telephone and utility bills are written in three or four languages. The telephone directory, Yellow Pages, advertises their Spanish edition. Mosques and temples and synagogues allow them to worship as their parents did, or more likely, our hedonistic culture leaves the younger generations in spiritual isolation and darkness.

I can drive less than two miles from our house and find myself an American minority. Beginning in 1975, Linda Vista, a community of San Diego, had 15-18,000 Southeast Asians trying to forget the horrors of Vietnam and Cambodia and establish new lives. Now their children and even grandchildren attempt to straddle the culture of two societies. The signs on their stores and restaurants don't speak *my* language! The cultures and languages of Southeast Asia still permeate the homes and neighborhoods, holding back those who would want to be "American."

On one occasion, so numerous were the people from one area of Cambodia that they went en masse to the San Diego City Council demanding that an old tribal chief of theirs be given a seat on the Council to represent them! They were given a quick lesson in civics. Just the thought of their proposal, however, should give us some idea of the extent to which some internationals are intending to maintain their cultural identity.

A few miles east, 4000 immigrants per month are swelling the population of the city of El Cajon. Only there the signs on stores and shops are in Arabic as these current refugees are coming from the terrors of the Middle East.

Amnesty, by whatever name you would call it and by the stroke of a president's pen, legalizes thousands of internationals to live among us. The aftermath of one or another "war on terrorism" allows people of all social and economic strata to enter our gates, take jobs and enjoy unquestioned freedoms. An overthrow of a government identifies additional thousands as "political" refugees. And the waters of "humanity in need" flood over the United States.

Whatever the motivation, there is more cross-cultural traveling, more movement of peoples today than at any previous time in history. Political, economic, educational, social and religious factors have promoted this unprecedented movement of people. Modern communication, a redistribution of world wealth and space age transportation have made it possible.

Everyone in America, in the course of time, will have to face living and relating with internationals. Many already are accepting the global village as an exciting new place to live. They are learning new values—where people are more important than production, for example. They are coming to appreciate exotic new foods. Some English speakers are even choosing to learn a second language, overcoming the widespread American "disease" of the tongue, mono-lingualism.

Others are trying to reject this *intrusion* and are trying to live in social and cultural isolation. Some are taking up one or another cause to fight the inevitable changing tide. A young man with a voice mature beyond his eleven years, sang the United States national anthem at the opening of an NBA playoff game. His voice resonated through the whole range of notes. You could see his heart swelling with pride with each crescendo. With tears welling up in his eyes, as he held onto the final note, he thrust his hand upward to the American flag. However, "Tweets" filled cyberspace as critics spit their venom of hatred for our ever-increasing multi-cultural society. "How can we let an illegal alien sing *our* national anthem?" questioned one tweeter.

Only time will tell the results of the course each of us chooses to take. In this book we want to address the issues of taking deliberate steps *now* to bridge the cultural distinctives of the internationals who live among us, to present a Savior in a context relevant to them.

In declaring his righteousness Job said, *"No stranger had to spend a night in the street, for my door was always open to the traveler"* (Job 31:32). Many years later the writer of Hebrews concluded his exhortation to Christians, *"Let brotherly love continue. Take care to keep your homes open to strangers, for men in their hospitality have, without knowing it, at times entertained angels"* (Hebrews 13:1-2).

The strangers in our midst are very open to hospitality
and have a great desire to meet Americans personally.
Many feel isolated and alone. For others, the foods and
customs are so different and difficult here in the USA.
The first time we took a Chinese friend to a Soup &
Salad restaurant, he thought he would "die" eating that
uncooked food! Most find the common usage of English
strangely unrelated to the textbook variety they might
have studied back home—especially our *wild & wooly*
idioms!

There are no less than seven distinct groups of
internationals living among us. They are here for a wide
variety of reasons. They got here by divergent means.
They have real ambitions. Yet, all have one need: A right
relationship with God through Jesus Christ, our Savior.

INTERNATIONAL STUDENTS

At any given time, there are over one million
international students from 181 countries studying in
the United States. They range from junior high through
university; they stay for two weeks to four years. They
have come to prepare for prominent positions in their
home countries. Many will become the world leaders
of tomorrow—in politics, war, economics, science,
education or religion.

Most of these students have never heard the Gospel.
Nearly half are from countries that have closed their doors
to Christian missionaries. Now God has brought them
here to live among us. He has given us the opportunity
to share His love and introduce them to Christ.

When international students arrive in America, they
have questioning minds and searching hearts. They
want to learn and experience all there is in this vast
country. They are lonely, vulnerable—open. What will fill
that void?

This is the perfect scenario for the entrance of a Christian with a global worldview. Internationals almost never refuse hospitality offered to them. They covet opportunities for friendship, especially if it's offered in the warm atmosphere of the living or dining room of a home. And how much better if it is in *your* Christian home!

More than just an ambassador of goodwill between nations, you are Christ's ambassador (II Corinthians 5:20), representing the Kingdom of God to one ensnared in the kingdom of darkness. A Christian who consistently and persistently befriends an international student may very well see his friend profess faith in Christ and return to his own people as a dynamic and effective witness.

There is a wide range of opportunities for ministry among international students. You can simply attend a potluck dinner sponsored by the local college (or by your church) welcoming new students to the USA or you can host a student in your home. You can simply give him a Scripture portion in his own language or you can commit to one-on-one discipling, preparing him for making an intentional spiritual impact when he goes home. When he returns, you can put other Christian ministries in that country in touch with him. He also becomes an *open door* for you to visit his country in the future.

The world is sending the cream of their youth to America for their education. You can make sure a part of that education includes exposure to and participation in the Kingdom of God.

MISSIONARY KIDS

Yes, you read that correctly: Missionary children! More specifically, children of career missionaries. Living among us is this unique group of internationals. Born to U.S. parents (at least one is a U.S. citizen); possibly born in the United States, but more likely not; raised in a second and third and possibly fourth culture, they come *home* one year in five. It is possible that by the time a missionary kid (MK) is eighteen (and supposedly prepared to take on adult responsibilities in his culture), he has been in his homeland for no more than three years! Once at five years old, again at ten, and once at fifteen years of age!

"Does he speak English?" the woman asked in a loud whisper, gesturing at the young man standing awkwardly in the foyer of the church after the morning service. He had heard her question but didn't know how to or *if* he should approach the ladies. In the culture in which he had grown up, men did not talk with women unless they were in the company of their male relatives. The woman's question implied more than an insult to his language ability. It suggested her own difficulty in knowing how to relate with a real, live adult missionary kid.

He had heard it was a good church. He had been challenged by the sermon. He had just arrived in this town to attend a nearby college. Classes hadn't started yet. This was his first Sunday "home." But, now what?

One girl graduated with every honor offered to a high school senior. Her college entrance exam scores assured her a choice of many universities. She could paddle a dugout canoe and swim like a fish. Yet, when she crossed the Los Angeles Air Terminal building, she saw a drinking fountain. (Because of *my* cross-cultural upbringing in Wisconsin, I still want to call those things "bubblers.") Standing in front of it, she didn't know how to turn it on! Nor did she have the "American ingenuity" to step aside and watch how someone else did. She went away thirsty.

College MK's have developed a loosely affiliated care group, MuKappa, the Greek letters for MK. Others have established adult care groups. Still others help non-MK spouses understand their mates! But there is room for you to befriend a bewildered MK who is coming to a college in your town, whose parents are remaining on their field of service.

ILLEGAL ALIENS

Whether it was the Amnesty Act of 1872 which re-enfranchised ex-confederates in hopes that they would vote for Democratic candidate Horatio Seymour over Republican Ulysses S. Grant or President Reagan's impassioned appeal for those "who had put down roots in America" or Bush's *temporary* amnesty for illegal immigrants or President Obama side-stepping Congress with his executive fiat, amnesty has not diminished the flow of new aliens crossing our borders illegally. Whatever name you choose—aliens, undocumented workers or illegal immigrants, efforts to stanch their flow have done exactly the opposite. If anything, these flawed plans have *encouraged* a greater influx of illegals.

Though from many other nations of origin, the nearly 2000-mile U.S./Mexico border is the border crossing of choice. Canada and the shores of the Atlantic and Pacific provide further access. According to a Pew Hispanic Center's estimate, illegal aliens represent one-third of the foreign-born population in America and cost American taxpayers 100 billion dollars a year.[3]

Not an Arizona sheriff, a "beefed-up" border patrol, a high wall topped with barbed wire, nor a vigilante neo-Nazi posse is going to keep them out. They are internationals who live among us. They are living throughout our country, not just in the southern States. Not unlike the brother and sister from Guatemala in the movie, *El Norte*, they have come from the north or south or east or west in quest of the "good life."[4]

An even greater number of illegal aliens are those who came legally...and just never went home! Yes, our great nation freely gives a six-month tourist visa to thousands every year, but our government's way of checking if/ when they leave is inadequate. Many just don't!

Under the fearful duress of being caught and deported, (by whatever means they got here), they are open to a new life in Christ that you can share with them: A life that transcends the mundane of this world and ushers them into the Kingdom of God. And when they are caught and bused to the border or put on a plane, you have just sent out your own missionaries!

INTERNATIONAL VISITORS

Whether you have the San Diego Zoo with an estimated 6,000 international visitors a day, or if yours is a quaint village that has preserved an early American folk dance that a group from Russia is coming to watch, there *are* international visitors in your home town!

They are the new wealthy of the Third World. They have heard incredible stories from their countrymen of the coast-to-coast *Disneyland*; they have seen "America" on *Dallas, CSI Criminal Investigations* and *Desperate Housewives*, the most-watched TV shows in the world! Do you wonder why they have a hard time believing that everyone doesn't live like that? Or do we, by comparison? For years they may have anticipated this visit of a lifetime—everything is so big, bright and glamorous to them! And they go home—empty still.

Unless...unless you are there...there to invite them for a visit in a *typical* Christian home! You can find them at your tourist attractions; you can find them through your Chamber of Commerce, visitor stations along the freeway, travel agencies and tourist offices. You can catch their distinctly different speech on every street corner.

My wife and I were at the beach watching the sea lions and the sunset with an international friend, visiting us from England. From across the walkway, a Chinese lady approached me, asking for the name of the big birds perched here and there. I responded, helping her teach that English word to her two children. Satisfied that they had mastered it, we went back to watching the sea lions. But my wife was impressed to strike up a further conversation with the lady: How long have you been here? Where are you from? Are you here on vacation? All the words to help develop rapport. And then...the question: Have you been able to visit in an American home yet? Would you like to?

They had been here for almost a month and only seldom had been away from the apartment they had rented. Nor had they related with the neighbors on a personal level. Again, my wife asked, "Would you like to visit an American home?" The lady jumped at the chance. They had not been in anyone's home all month. A date was set. We invited our granddaughter to join us. She had interest in ministering in China.

My wife fixed a typical American meatloaf, baked potatoes, vegetable and salad dinner. We all held hands as I offered a prayer. The Chinese lady showed a respectful acceptance of that. But, they had never seen such big potatoes! They had never eaten a baked potato! The mother devoured hers. Her young son, not able to eat all of his, had left half of it on his plate. Mom asked us if it would be okay for her to finish his! I am sure she had a big "tummy ache" after she left! We enjoyed a lot of laughs. No "Bible-thumping" sermons—just a friendly visit. Out of that visit, our granddaughter was given an invitation to the lady's home in China to help her improve her Chinese language skills. Just three extra places at a meal table and Seeds of the Gospel were sown.

We also were able to put her in touch with a Chinese-speaking church in San Diego, which they visited. In turn, the pastor gave her a connection with a church in China for when they return home. What eternal ramifications? Only eternity will tell!

They are internationals who live among us, too. They are here so briefly, but how long does it take to sense sincere friendliness? A relationship can then develop by correspondence. Neither prayer nor the Word of God is bound by time and space. Anyway, *"one plants, another waters, but God gives the increase"* (I Corinthians 3:7).

INTERNATIONAL BUSINESS PEOPLE

International business people, already in places of leadership in their own countries, are in the USA typically for short stays. They are here buying up our forests, our scrap metal, or our real estate! Some are guest lecturers at our universities. Others are diplomats, involved in some government-relations capacity. Others are with their country's military or are seafarers. Still others are learning techniques in one or another of our industries.

They, too, are lonely. They are usually here without family and are open to friendships. I was speaking on this theme at a church in Oxnard, California some time ago. One seminar participant told this story:

> I was working as a custodian at a local hotel that had been purchased by an electronics firm. Every three months a new group of men from the Middle East arrived to learn how to operate equipment their country had purchased. They were bused to the plant in the morning and back to the hotel at night. I had made some attempts at being friendly. But one evening, I was startled as an Iraqi grabbed me by the lapels of my shirt and pleaded, "Please invite me to your house for dinner!"

That begging was definitely out of context with his home culture, yet being so desperate for a friend, he let his need blurt out such a request.

You can invite them to your house for dinner! You can help them with their English. You can give them a tour of your city. You may even be able to introduce them to a *"Friend who sticks closer than a brother"* (Proverbs 18:24).

RELOCATING REFUGEES

The media spotlights have been turned OFF the global problem of relocating refugees for a long time. In the mid-70's you would have thought it to be the only group of uncared-for people in the world. Even Christian ministries, previously uncommitted to Southeast Asia, were riding the waves of popularity the boat people were giving to this need.

And I do not deny the devastation of that time. I wrote of my 1980 visit to a refugee holding center just inside the Thai border:

> We went to Enn Kiry's home. It was a six by ten foot bamboo shelf under a thatched roof shared with seven other family members. It was separated from the block-long row of identical "homes" by sheets of thatched bamboo leaves. One side was open to the cook fire on the ground.
>
> He said that throughout the night screams are heard all over the camp as one and another is awakened by the nightmarish memories of their escape. They sit up, cross-legged, shivering in the hot night air, reliving the anguish of their past: Grandparents who were left in the ditch to die because they could not keep up with the fleeing group; babies who died of malnutrition in the arms of their mothers who had no milk to give; sisters who were kidnapped and raped, then cut in half with a machete; merciless torture—sex organs cut off and eaten by Polpot's soldiers; slow

acting poison put in their rice, so thousands died three months later; the anxiety of not knowing if one or another family member made it to safety. The atrocities of man against man! May God have mercy on us and give us His wisdom!

And of our 1988 visit to KAI TAK Vietnamese Refugee Camp in Hong Kong, I wrote:

> Five thousand people were "warehoused" in 4'x4'x8' cubicles stacked two high and six deep. Cotton cloth on drawstrings separated each family's quarters from the next. Three long buildings of these metal and plywood "apartments" entombed the solemn heartaches of displaced families.
>
> Ngan, a six-year internee of this camp (another year at a previous one), led to the Lord by our friend, Darren, said he would escape again! Indicating that seven years of this is better than what he left. My heart breaks for refugees!

But today, there is an annual United Nations High Commission for Refugees World Refugee Day, so designated by a UN resolution in 2001. It took me a Google search to discover that there is one. And another two clicks to find its date! Do you know the date? Where were you on June 20th? I was celebrating our daughter's birthday! Who even gave thought to the significance of that day in relationship to refugees?

But today, though little is heard of their plight, located around the world in some country that knows no better than another how to deal with this problem, in conditions no better than the ones described, languish 45.7 million refugees (2012).[5]

But today, 80% of the world's refugees are women and children, many of whom have been displaced by armed conflict. Men and boys have been conscripted into armies or killed. The genocide attempts in the Nuba Mountains of Sudan, Darfur, Somalia, Afghanistan, and Palestine have become *household words* representing a world gone wrong. Others are only known by searching the Internet: The Rohingya and Karen people of Burma face the genocidal forces of a military regime.[6]

But today, what is known of the hurting individuals caught in the ugliness of ideological and physical warfare? Every minute of every day, eight people decide to leave everything behind to escape war, persecution or terror. The choice is brutal: either stay and risk your life as whole villages are systematically bombed or flee and face the risk of kidnap, rape, or torture.

But today, for some who stayed, a news headline that will be forgotten tomorrow: *Fifty people ran to their pastor's home, only to be surrounded by their persecutors. The house was torched. No survivors.*

But today, for some who fled, a news headline that will be forgotten tomorrow: *Sri Lankan authorities have arrested another 41 would-be illegal immigrants heading to Australia.*

But today, refugees are *NOT* statistics! They are men and women, boys and girls, many of whom have never seen what's on the other side of that 15-foot block wall topped with some spiral of barbed wire. Whole generations of refugees are now born in camps. Children and grandchildren of those who fled have never seen their homeland. Stories of life *before* have faded. Without any prospect of hope for the future, they are destined to a life without meaning. Only two percent are slated for resettlement or return to their homeland. The rest remain in limbo. Waiting.... Wondering.... Hoping....

But today, the plight of many refugees does not end when they are relocated. Sometimes insensitive to what refugees have experienced before arriving, the host country violates deep cultural distinctives; sometimes scheming attorneys, real estate brokers, doctors or car sales people deliberately exploit and rip them off. Store clerks become impatient with their lack of knowledge of coins and just grab them out of their hand. (I saw this happen in a store in San Diego. After the customer left, I said, "It is too bad no one has taken the time to teach her about American coins." The clerk's response: An unmentionable curse!)

But today, Christians can expend their energy debating the social injustice issues that definitely cloud the refugee problem. Or, you can respond to Jesus' Words, *"I was a stranger and you took Me in"* (Matthew 25:35).

ETHNIC COMMUNITIES

Thousands of internationals every year are granted permanent residence. They differ from *international students* in that they are staying. They differ from *relocating refugees* in that they come voluntarily. They differ from *international business people* in that they are setting up businesses here. They differ from *international visitors* in that they will visit their homeland after they have been successful here.

They cluster into communities where they can sense the familiar; where they can feel a security from those *others* out there; where they are *at home*. Not only are they not amalgamating into the steel of America but also fear and suspicion of other Third World ethnic communities keep them isolated from each other. "We have nothing to do with the Mexicans here," sneers Arturo Price of Colombia. "Our culture is different; our Spanish is more pure."

A community of 5000 Mayans from one village in Guatemala now lives in Los Angeles. The original village no longer exists.

When the children are gathered into one classroom, the admixture is not much better. A teacher friend of mine said she spends the first several days just trying to identify who can understand whom, and who can best help whom to understand the *English* instructions!

Demographers do their surveys and quilt a patchwork pattern on their charts reducing to statistics the divergent locations and needs of these *aliens* in our land. We must never look at them as so many numbers on a computer-generated graph! We must reach out to them with our heart of love and our hand of friendship.

Yes, each of these groups is dramatically different from the others, requiring a careful consideration of our approach in evangelism. Yet, they are so much alike. For in the heart (or throat or liver or spleen, depending on their home culture) of each one is a God-shaped vacuum that can be filled by none other than God, Himself. Thus, we want to *"open their eyes, turn them from darkness to light, from the power of satan to God, so that they may receive forgiveness of sins, and be given a place among God's people who are sanctified by faith that is in Me"* (Acts 26:18).

Christian, one of the most strategic "foreign" mission fields today is at the very doorstep of your home.

- Strategic because it is so close at hand. *They* have moved into *your* neighborhood.
- Strategic because it represents the segment of our population with the most dramatic growth.
- Strategic because it does not cost the "mega-bucks" of going to another country.
- Strategic because it is good training for those who *will* go to another country.
- Strategic because so little effort yields such a great harvest.
- Strategic because it reaches people who are open to the Gospel. They are open to the Gospel

because they are in the disadvantaged position of being the *foreign* one. They are open to the Gospel because they have left their country (often) under the duress of political, economic or religious oppression. They are open to the Gospel because, for all of the negative rhetoric about a "Godless" America, when they come here they see the outpouring of God's blessing on a nation that is still largely honoring God!

• Strategic because it is in His Word: *"Do not take advantage of aliens in your land; do not wrong them. They must be treated like any other citizen: Love them as yourself..."* (Leviticus 19:33-34).

By way of introduction to the wide-open door of ministry to internationals who live among us, what more needs to be said? Only this:

The frontiers of world evangelization are not only in Tibet, Saudi Arabia, Mozambique and China. The frontiers of unreached people groups are also in Boston, New York, Chicago, San Diego and _____! (*Name your town.*) God has brought the internationals of the world to the doorstep of every church and neighborhood in America! Let's do world missions at home!

In the following chapters, we want to explore in greater detail the challenges and opportunities with each of these groups of internationals who live among us.

BUILDING BRIDGES TO
INTERNATIONAL STUDENTS 2

PLEASE, LET ME STAY LONGER

A chef prepared Arthur Lim's meals. A chauffeur drove him wherever he pleased; servants attended to his needs. But when Arthur left his home in Singapore to study in California, he had to function on his own—and that was a bit scary. He became homesick and missed his long talks with his mother.

How thankful Arthur was when Sam, a worker with an international student ministry, arranged for him to stay for two weeks with a family, Leonard and Joyce Sutton.

After his stay ended, Arthur pleaded with Leonard and Joyce, "I have become so attached to your family— please, let me stay longer! My father will pay whatever it costs you. I will even prepare my own meals!"

Arthur became a permanent member of the family, taking part in all family activities. Although he attended church at first only because the family did, Arthur continued attending because of the love and care he felt there.

That summer the church college group planned a singing and witnessing trip to Washington State. Arthur had attended their Bible study and wanted to go on the trip.

"You may go along," the youth pastor said, "if I may talk to you daily about the Lord."

Arthur eagerly agreed, and returned from the trip excited to learn more about God. A month later he professed his new faith in Christ and was baptized.

When Arthur transferred to San Francisco State University, he began teaching a Bible study in Mandarin for college students. He also joined a hospital visitation program through his new church. During the hospital visits, Arthur met Polly, a Christian from Taiwan whose testimony touched his heart. They married after graduation from college and returned to Singapore.

Arthur continued with the Lord in Singapore, becoming a deacon and a worker in the church's high school ministry. "When the students advanced to college," says Leonard, "Arthur's ministry did too! It is so rewarding to see Arthur's dedication to the Lord. Young people who have come out of Buddhism are such strong witnesses to their friends, family and community."

A while ago Arthur and Polly started a church called True Grace. More than 100 college-age people attend, most of them from Buddhist backgrounds.

Sam, who has visited the Lim home in Singapore, says, "Every evening Arthur and Polly spend two hours discipling students. We were thrilled to see their enthusiasm to reach out to college students and colleagues."[1]

Arthur's story has been repeated numerous times in the "Raj's", the "Yuko's" and the "Isabel's" of the international student community. They met people committed to reaching out in friendship to students of other countries. The sincere "no-strings-attached" friendships developed into caring relationships. The incarnational love of Jesus Christ became infectious. In their openness to the Gospel, new life was born in their hearts.

Unfortunately, all stories are not so positive. While here, many of these future leaders have experienced cold treatment, discrimination and rejection instead of a warm welcome and God's love. Consequently, many have returned to their countries as enemies of America and America's Christianity. When they rose to positions of influence, they did everything they could to close the door to missionaries. We can only wish that Gandhi and Ho Chi Min and many leaders like them had returned to their countries as followers of Christ to influence their own people for Christ.

Jonathan's eyes gleamed with anticipation as he prepared to travel to America to study political science. His hard work in his home country had paid off. An academic fellowship would pay all his school and living expenses for four years. He then could expect a prominent government position in his own country.

But during his four years in the United States, Jonathan wanted to mingle with Americans. He was eager to make friends, explore the country, learn to eat the food, understand the culture. He also hoped to meet a family who would take the place of his own on holidays and school vacations. And Christianity? Jonathan had heard such conflicting opinions about it that he wanted to meet someone who could give him a real insider's view. This was an ideal time to explore it, he realized, before he settled down with a job and family.

Jonathan's university was an excellent one and his professors were encouraging. But mostly his experience in America was disappointing. Like many other students who come to America, he was soon deeply disillusioned.

People seemed completely indifferent to his presence. Although fellow students greeted him politely and occasionally asked him about home, none invited him out or seriously tried to befriend him.

He immersed himself in his studies, but holidays were lonely and empty. His interest in the culture and religion of this country faded as he came to feel that its people were uncaring, arrogant, insincere. He forced himself to stay the four years, dreaming only of the day he would return to his home country and do his best to forget his unhappy sojourn in America.[2]

During the 1920s, Yosuki Matsuoki, from Japan, came to Portland, Oregon, and studied at a university. While in the U.S., Matsuoki felt poorly treated. He returned home hateful and embittered about America. Over time, he rose through the ranks of power. Finally he got his revenge on the American people when he assisted in the planning and execution of the Japanese attack on Pearl Harbor. The course of history might have been different during the 1940s if that lonely student had been befriended by loving Christians twenty years earlier.[3]

THEY ARE HERE...THEY ARE OPEN...THEY NEED A FRIEND

From nearly every country in the world, at any given time, there are living among us over one million international students. The world is sending the cream of their youth to America for their education. These students are their countries' brightest and most promising. They are being trained for leadership positions back home. Yet most have never even heard the Gospel. In fact, nearly half of these students are from the more than 55 nations that have closed their doors to missionaries. Some of the most influential people of tomorrow's world have moved in right next door to you.

Since the Second World War, thousands of them have been coming to America for higher studies and professional experience with the intention of returning to their countries with the academic and professional knowledge gained here. They have become leaders in every level of national influence.

For perspective, consider this: Imagine a city the size of San Francisco populated entirely by future global leaders. While its citizens come from almost every nation on earth, they all speak, or are quickly learning, English.

The boundaries of this city likely reach all the way to your doorstep. Then imagine that in four years, most of this city's population will be gone, but another 800,000-plus new citizens will take their place. This "city" is the university-level international student population studying right now in our country.

Many sincere church leaders are concerned about the doors being closed abroad for foreign missions. The puzzling thing, however, is that the majority of them have been missing the obvious open door to the world of nations through the visiting international students right at their doorstep.

Thankfully, the situation is changing. More and more churches are now realizing their opportunity to do *foreign* missions at home. For Christians, these visiting internationals represent one of the most strategic mission fields of our time since they come from so many nations of the world, including the "closed" nations. What a tremendous opportunity we have to fulfill the Great Commission by reaching these visiting internationals right here with the Gospel and sending them back as missionaries to their own people! I hope you are excited about this *foreign* mission field that has come to us. For, the key to reaching them is *YOU!*

I AM AN INTERNATIONAL STUDENT

"Have you ever met an international student? Have you ever talked to one? Has one ever talked to you? May I introduce myself? I represent one million people from junior high through university age from nearly every country in the world who are in the United States and many millions more who have returned to their respective homelands. I have already experienced the best my country offers. My family is socially well respected and economically well to do. I have had a good education. Now I am here to enhance it with what your country has to offer me. In most instances I represent the future leaders of the world. In this decade several million of us will take influential positions in politics, military, economics, science, education or religion.

"People often ignore me, mostly in ignorance of not knowing how to relate to me. Some openly reject me, revealing the prejudice that separates nations and people. Others give me a hearing (as you are), and accept the challenge I represent.

"I came to America lonely, vulnerable, and ill at ease in a culture vastly different from mine. The food and customs were difficult to adjust to. My body was not immune to the impurities in your water. The fast-paced lifestyle of America still makes me dizzy. Slow down, please! I need some time for reflection! But you don't slow down; nor can I!

"I came from a family-centered society. The individualistic society of the United States alienates me. I can't find a place to 'fit in.' I am many thousands of miles from my family and friends. I am still lonely.

"When school is on, my studies keep me challenged. I could use some help with reading my homework. But holidays are hard. Your holidays don't have much meaning for me, and while you're busy enjoying them, I feel particularly isolated. Then, when *my* holidays come and you ignore them, the hurt is very deep, but suffered alone. I know you don't understand.

"English language was a requirement in my country. Knowing I would come to America, I worked hard at it. But I found that the common usage of *American* English was quite unrelated to the book variety I studied. And especially your *wild & wooly* idioms!

"Then when you do discover that I am struggling to understand your language, please don't raise your voice. Saying words I don't understand in a louder voice doesn't help—though I know that is a typical reaction. Slowing down a bit would help. Using simpler words to say the same thing would be good. Giving me the time to look up words on my iPhone would also help.

"The vast majority of us—acknowledging that we are guests in your country—are friendly and polite. We are diligent, serious-minded and ambitious. Most of us are eager to know about your culture. Without your help, though, many of us have a hard time distinguishing between Christianity, Americanism, and capitalism, mixed with your move toward socialism. It is easy in our rejection of one to simply reject them all. But we want to know...we *do* want to know about your Christian faith. I will accept a Bible. And I will read it! An impressive number of us are willing to spend hours (maybe even more than you want to) talking about the Christian faith. Especially if it is in the warm atmosphere of the living or dining room of your home!

"We're here. We're living among you. The reasons for which we came are diverse. Some are noble; some motives are not so pure. But we're here. What are *you* going to do with me? Well, not me. But the others.... You see, I am one of the fortunate few who has recently found a friend in America. Oh, here he comes now. Let me introduce him to you. This is Jonathan."

"Hi! Yes, I grew up in a church that emphasized missions. Speakers came from distant lands telling of the challenge to reach the lost. My heart was stirred with compassion, so I began praying for various missionaries. But I wanted to have a more direct contact with people of other cultures—with internationals. Yet, circumstances of my life would not allow me to travel to those distant lands I had heard about.

"One day I opened my eyes to realize that God has brought the internationals of the world to the doorstep of every church in America! Now we have opened the door of our home and our hearts to international students. We are involved! What a great pleasure! What an opportunity God has put before us. 'It's better than a day at the beach,' I realized after my first contact with an international student. My wife says it makes her feel like 'an ambassador with a teacup!'"

Ambassador, indeed—and for the sake of Christ! A Christian who consistently and persistently befriends an international student may very well see his friend profess faith in Christ and return to his own people as a dynamic and effective witness.

Jonathan continues, "Entertaining international students makes a tremendous impact on our whole family, as well. A part of the distant world comes right into our home. Our children develop a rich sense of appreciation for the peoples and cultures of other countries. Our interest in the _mission_ of the church broadens remarkably. The world _over there_ becomes flesh and blood. Life in Amman, Bangkok and Brasilia becomes a personal prayer concern for us because our friends—international students who lived with us, who shared their lives with us—are now back home in those places. The work of Christ in other lands becomes more significant and more personal."

Of course, most international students come here thinking that everyone in America is a Christian, and that our society with its crime and divorce must be a result of our religion. Where do they get such a warped concept? From _CSI Investigations_, the most-watched TV show in the world. From stories told them by others who have been here. From international news. Their concepts will be a composite of truth, misunderstanding and stereotypes of falsehood!

"Will these visitors enjoy coming into my home, then?" you may ask. If you were 5000 miles away from your home and family, wouldn't you be thrilled to accept an invitation into a home with sincere warmth like yours has? These students miss their families. They are also curious about your furnace and what's in the attic. As they look at your "stuff" in the garage, they ask, "And you rent a storage unit, too?" Don't be surprised at any question. Learn to "read between the lines" of what they say. Don't take anything for granted.

But, on the other hand, these internationals are not so interested in your furnishings, your *original* art, or your silverware. After all, half the world eats (very artistically) with their fingers, one-fourth with chopsticks, and only one-fourth with silverware. So, a formal setting of sterling may not impress but rather only frustrate your visitor! They want to know *you*—they need *your* friendship—regardless of the elegance of your belongings. Does this going back and forth sound a bit ambiguous? Well, it will be good for you to get comfortable with a lot of uncertainty. They will present you with as many surprises as you give to them!

One host family developed a real friendship with Raj from India. One night they got an unexpected invitation and couldn't get a babysitter for their young children. They called Raj and asked him if he would babysit. He gladly agreed because he loved the children. The parents had been out of the house only ten minutes or so when the phone rang. The person on the line asked to speak with the father. Raj explained, "I am sorry, but he just passed away." After a sustained silence, the party finally asked to speak with the mother. Raj answered, "I am sorry, she passed away also. They passed away together about ten minutes ago!"

"Our kids look forward to having internationals visit our home. Our son saw me pulling into the driveway with an international student. He turned to his mother with a disappointed look and said, 'Aw, only one!' Rely on your children as wonderful icebreakers. Who can resist a little 'ankle-biter' climbing up on his knee? Or an ambitious eight year old explaining the wonders of model airplanes? Our kids enjoy showing our scrapbooks and talking with internationals about—everything! Both children feel at home in our world because so much of the world has been in our home! Internationals especially enjoy the very young and the very old. They miss children and grandparents so very much while they are here. And they look on the aged with a respect too often forgotten by Americans. We are grateful that the Lord directed my family to minister to international students who live among us."[4]

But many of the international students do not embrace the Christian faith. It is still important to love them, to pray for them, and to continue the friendship after they return home. Correspondence and exchange of visits are very possible in our world. You may see some professing faith in Christ years later; but even if that doesn't transpire, the value of the friendship is immeasurable. They continue to be a bridge to an important part of God's world. They are at least ambassadors of the goodwill they experienced in the United States. And those who choose to be ambassadors for Christ are better equipped to carry out His commission as nationals working among their own people. Throughout the world today, men and women who were touched by His Spirit through caring Americans, are serving Christ in their own country, where they know the language and culture. They are at home and winning many to Christ.

Just one more story to challenge you that it can be done—that *you* can do it!

A young child psychiatrist, Bronson Stilwell, and his wife, Evelyn, were living the normal American lifestyle. As newlyweds, they had explored a future with Wycliffe but were eventually persuaded to pursue a mission that might possibly utilize his new profession. They and their young family settled on the outskirts of a small college town.

During this time, they enrolled in the Perspectives Course, an excellent study[5] used to open their eyes to a ministry they had never considered—international students. These students were arriving at the college campus in their town lost in an ocean of newness— new language, culture, and relationships. Bronson and Evelyn tested the waters by working with the campus office to pick up new students at the airport and help with orientation activities. Meeting and assisting these grateful and charming students proved to be rewarding for their whole family.

The Stilwells began dreaming about a building right across from the university campus that had been vacant for some time. After being broken up into apartments over the years and serving as a fraternity house, not many people were willing to tackle the enormous remodeling project. Bronson and Evelyn, though, saw the potential of having space to live, work, and invite international students to live alongside of them. There was a lot of hammering, sawing, and painting, but soon the dream became a reality. They moved in and the students followed.

"Would you like to come and cook a meal typical of your country?" became a regular invitation quickly embraced by those being invited on Sunday afternoons. Word traveled by word-of-mouth and students began moving into the remodeled apartments and agreed to the expectations of eating with all the residents Monday through Thursday evenings and joining a weekly Bible discussion. Love and respect for each other grew during these times and many decided to embrace Jesus' offer of redemption that they discovered through the discussion and the love they experienced there.[6]

The Stilwells demonstrated just how far love would go to woo people from every tongue, tribe, and nation into His kingdom. They knit their hearts together with people from around the world who moved into their world, realizing more deeply than ever that they are "blessed to be a blessing." (See Psalm 67:1-2.)

HOW NOT TO WELCOME INTERNATIONAL STUDENTS

While in Asia I met a university student who was coming to America to further her education. I told her I would try to put her in touch with a church in the area where she was going. When I got home I called a pastor. He was enthusiastic about helping. I was sure this would be a good connection. His email to her follows:

> Hi Ana (all names and locations have been changed to protect the innocent and guilty),
>
> My name is Joe Smith, and I pastor (name of church and website). Neal has been trying to put us all in touch during your stay here in America, so I wanted to send you an invitation to come and join our fellowship sometime soon. The website has all the details you will need, but we meet on Sunday mornings at 10:30 in Morristown, and you can even take the Metro to the church—it's the Morristown Station on the Green Line. We also have at least two people in the church who speak Mandarin and would love to meet you and help you in any way possible.
>
> We look forward to seeing you soon, and if there is anything we can do to help with your stay in Morristown, please just ask.
>
> Blessings in Christ,
> JS
> (church phone number)

Needless to say, we found another church for her!

BUILDING BRIDGES TO INTERNATIONAL STUDENTS

Certainly, our primary concern is for the salvation of the lost. However, evangelism and friendship go hand in hand! Evangelism has three steps: plowing, planting, and reaping.

Planting is the step of sharing the Gospel with them. However, sharing the Gospel is not just explaining the plan of salvation as found in so many Western Gospel presentations: the Four Spiritual Laws, the Roman Road or even the Scripture in I Corinthians 15:3-4: *"Christ died for our sins, fulfilling the Scriptures, was buried and on the third day, rose, fulfilling the Scriptures."* Usually it must be shared even more simply, showing them who Christ is, possibly beginning with the Scripture, *"Don't be afraid! Listen, I bring you great news of tremendous joy, which is for all people. For this very day, in the city of David, a Savior has been born for you. He is Christ the Lord"* (Luke 2:10,11). Or, at an even more basic level for many cultures, beginning with, "In the beginning..." (Genesis 1).

Since international students come from backgrounds with different concepts of God, sin and salvation, it is unwise to assume that they automatically understand the Christian doctrines. So we must explain the Gospel in a way that they understand clearly. *"But he who received the Seed on the good ground is he who hears the Word and understands it"* (Matthew 13:23). This requires knowledge of their background as well as our ability to explain the Gospel at a level deep enough to reach these intellectuals. Helping them to see who Christ is in reality is vitally important since that is the basis of making a life-long commitment to Him. And we need to be able to do this without using our "Christianese" language! Also, people of various cultures and languages develop thought patterns somewhat different from ours. We must carefully listen and try to understand what they say about what they are understanding about what we are trying to say. And if that statement got twisted around in your mind, you are beginning to understand the difficulty of cross-cultural communication! And it goes a lot deeper than avoiding telling a Hindu, "You must be born again!"

Reaping is the step of leading them to a commitment to Christ. Of first consideration, we must realize that plowing, planting and reaping are not likely to happen all on the same day. Elementary as this truth is, many who share Christ with internationals expect a commitment immediately. We are used to seeing immediate commitments being made in crusades, so we forget the truth that those who responded had probably already been "plowed and planted."

We cannot, however, assume this with international students. Internationals often want to oblige out of politeness, so pressuring them to pray the commitment prayer could result in their praying with you without heart commitment. This is counter-productive. Planting and reaping are possible only after a time of plowing.

Plowing is the step of preparing the ground—their hearts—for receiving the Gospel message. Plowing arouses their curiosity to hear the Gospel; it softens their hearts to receive the Seed of the Word. This comes through building enduring friendships. Christian friendship *is* the plowing step.

International students are mostly unplowed ground. Most of them come from the background of other religions and philosophies, and cultures that know little to nothing of the Judeo-Christian ethic. They may be satisfied with their religion. Some of them may have misconceptions about Christianity. Others may be skeptical towards all religions as a result of their secular studies. Many international students arrive in America with the impression that America is a Christian nation and that most Americans are Christians. However, almost everything they see and experience here—in their universities, in the media, in society, in the church itself—may cause them to change that view. They may develop a very negative attitude towards Christianity. They may also observe that Christianity is not seriously followed by those who call themselves Christians and thus come to the conclusion that it is not worth seriously looking into, or that Christianity is not good enough. The unfriendliness they may experience from Christians and churches would only confirm their conclusions. How, then, do we get their attention to examine the claims of Christ?

Your international friend's exposure to *your* Christian lifestyle and faith is a key factor in arousing his interest in Christ, but that is going to happen only if you commit yourself to a long-standing, quality relationship. The opportunity to witness—that is, to show and tell about Christ in your life—will arise naturally again and again in your contacts. Surely the special holiday times of Christmas or Easter and at weddings or funerals or the miracle of birth of your second child or the beauty of a budding rose will give you opportunity to share Christ. However, he will more deeply find Christ in the demonstration of your belief in absolute Truth, including how it applies to all of the practical aspects of your life and relationships. Speaking that Truth in love with gentleness and respect will win their attention. With your caring love for them supporting what you tell them verbally, the Holy Spirit will arouse their curiosity to know about your attractive faith. This is the basic step in plowing.

The parable of the Sower (Matthew 13) explains clearly that for a good harvest, the Seed must be planted in plowed ground. The wonderful thing about this opportunity is that just about everybody can offer friendship. You don't have to be a professional missionary to be a friend with an international student.[7]

Listen to Matt's story:

Adeem dropped out of university and went straight to work. His job required him to make runs for spare parts whenever needed. Because of the tendency for sand storms in that area of the country, the company policy was that these outings should always be done in teams of two. This particular day, however, was especially busy, and Adeem wasn't able to find someone to accompany him.

The sand storm came out of nowhere, flipping Adeem's car and leaving him unconscious. He woke up in the hospital two days later surrounded by his boss and parents who had flown in to be by his side. Nobody could figure out how he was found or how he got to the hospital—but there he was! This was the first powerful indication that Someone, somewhere was looking out for him. The tilling of Adeem's soul had begun.

After recovering from the accident, Adeem moved home with his parents and decided to go back to college. He even started to make plans to study abroad, which is when he met his first Christian friend: his foreign English teacher. Although this friend wasn't able to see fruit in Adeem's life, seeds of the Gospel were planted. Several years and several thousand miles later, Adeem ended up on a university campus in Oregon.

Four months after his arrival in the U.S., Adeem finally got the courage to approach his instructor after class and ask, "How can I become a Christian?" Having figured that all Americans were Christians, this didn't strike Adeem as a strange question. His instructor, who was not a Christian, passed him along to an administrator who then sent an e-mail to me. I met Adeem for a cup of coffee and introduced him to Jesus. I thought, 'God is bringing students to the U.S. ready to receive Him!' It was in the months that followed that I was able to hear his whole story. The soil of Adeem's soul had gone through the difficult plowing and planting process before we had even met.[8]

ON BEING A FRIEND

The basic ingredient to friendship is love, for love involves acceptance, interest in the other person, and a willingness to meet that person's needs. People usually choose their friends based on common interests and agreeable qualities. The love of this type of friendship is conditional. It discriminates. The Greek word for it is *phileo.*

Christian friendship, however, should not be limited to those with agreeable qualities. God's command to us is to *"Love your neighbor as yourself"* (Matthew 19:19). The love here is *agape,* which is unconditional and all-inclusive.

Christians who are filled with God's agape love should be able to reach out to all internationals in friendship, regardless of their color, culture, race, or religion. Remember that the international is different in so many ways: physical appearance, dress, food habits, political views, sports interests, customs and manners, family living style, religion, work habits, language, names and taboos. These are basic cultural distinctives.

Accepting international students involves accepting them as fellow human beings of equal worth, though different in so many ways. There is no room for a superiority attitude.

Besides acceptance, friendship involves interest in the other person. This includes getting to know them. One of the most effective ways of getting to know others is through communication. Get them to talk about themselves. Ask them questions about themselves. Tell them about yourself, also. Here's how:

- Briefly describe yourself to them by the cultural distinctives just mentioned. What makes *you* a cultural being?
- Think of your international friend and describe how he is different from you in these same areas.
- Write down 15 (dialogue style) questions that you can ask an international whom you have met and want to know more deeply.
- Get to know some of the greetings in different languages. You will instantly get their attention if you will greet them in their own language.
- Learn to accurately pronounce their names.

Christians can often be aware only of the spiritual needs of others. So they rush to share the Gospel with them or take them to church. But, we must remember that Christian love cares for all needs, not just spiritual. *"I was thirsty and you gave Me a drink"* (Matt 25:35). Often the felt needs of people are not the spiritual needs. We can start at their felt needs and move towards their spiritual needs. Of course, if they cry out when they enter your home, "What must I do to be saved?" don't run to the kitchen to get them a drink of water!

Friendship is the single most important step in reaching an international student. For many, this country is strange and confusing. They need friends to help them through all sorts of cultural adjustments and such practical matters as renting an apartment or buying a car. It is fun to be that kind of friend. It can even be the beginning of a life-long relationship.

The ways to demonstrate this friendship are as limitless as the creative genius of God working through you. But, for starters, here are a few:

- Meet arriving students at the airport.
- Make sure they have housing from the first day.
- Help them secure permanent housing—maybe yours!
- Help them secure furnishings and get settled in their home.
- Utilities, telephone, bedding...
- Take them shopping for food and personal items.
- Point out the economical stores.
- Show them how to sort through all the ads, Craig's List and E-Bay.
- Provide them with a city map and bus schedules.
- Help them rent or buy a car.
- Coach them for their driver's license test.
- Take them on a tour of the city to orientate them.
- Help them find the post office, police station, laundromat...
- Help them purchase a cell phone or a chip for theirs.
- Take them to a bank to set up an account, checks, ATM card...
- Invite them home for meals.
- Sponsor or attend activities (picnics, retreats, sporting events, sight-seeing tours, zoo visits, museums).
- Pray for them—daily!
- Tutor them in conversational English.
- Visit them in their apartment and meet their friends; invite their friends over to your home.
- Have them babysit your children, after trust has been established, of course, and remember Raj's experience!
- Help them find part time jobs, if they may legally work.
- Write to their parents telling them about how/ what they are doing and what you have been

doing with them. You probably will need help writing in their language.

- Have your children write to their younger brothers and sisters, other family members.
- When he moves out of your area, continue praying for him and writing to him.
- Invite him to civic and church luncheons, banquets, beach parties and other activities.
- Let him help with things in the home.
- Share in his problems and needs. Have a good listening ear.
- Make your home a place to relax and rest—a HOME away from home.[9]

GETTING STARTED

The best way to make an initial contact is a Google search of the foreign students office of a college or university near you. Or the local high school district office. You can ask to be part of a welcoming group. You can ask for an international student of your preference (age, nationality, gender, interests, etc.) through the hospitality program to mentor or host in your home.

You can also meet internationals in the international programs on campus. Go to an international coffee hour or cultural event on campus. Visit with them briefly and invite them to your home for a meal. It is preferable that you arrange to pick them up at a specified place and time. In inviting girls, it is good to have a girl or couple to go and pick them up. Internationals are not used to going out one-on-one with the opposite sex. They may misunderstand such situations. Remember, *they* are the ones who are in an unfamiliar country. This first contact is very powerful in your friendship with internationals. It will form a bond of dynamic significance for your further interaction.

Internationals appreciate long-standing deep friendships, so choose carefully with how many you can relate. Bring them frequently to your home for meals, entertainment, sports events. And invite them to your church. Make them feel a part of your family. International students are used to the whole family being around from grandparents to grandchildren. Children are good bridges to friendship. Introduce your new friends to other Christians, especially others from the same campus. Call them at least once every week or two, but be sensitive to their class and study time. Ask them about their home and studies. Visit them in their place of residence.

Food is an important link in home hospitality. Internationals miss their home country food. If you know some international recipes, great! Otherwise you may know an international from the same country who will come and cook a dish at your place for your guest. Or, invite the students to cook their favorite meal for you. Shopping together for the necessary foods and seasonings will in itself be a great time of friendship building. This does require a bit of homework! Who doesn't eat pork? Who doesn't eat beef? Is chicken the *safest* meat? Who doesn't eat any meat? Be sensitive to this and make sure there are other food items. Be careful what you serve them. With some cultures it is even important in what pans you cook the food. Unfortunately, one international guest of ours discovered an authentic restaurant of her country's food. After that she didn't want to eat *our* food—ever again!

Help with conversational English is a valuable bridge. No degree is needed—anyone can do it! Internationals just need a model. Don't forget the international student's wife and family. Meeting once a week for an hour of English conversation practice can develop into a good friendship. It is important to use simple English as you talk with them; also, to speak slowly. Make sure they understand you by asking them questions.

One mentor expressed her excitement after her one semester commitment:

> I am not sure who benefits more from the tutor-mentor program, the student or the mentor. By meeting someone from another culture who is striving to speak and understand the English language, I find myself questioning not only what I say, but why I say the things I do. I have looked at our expressions with humor and confusion. When I struggle to explain what an idiom or euphemism means, I am struck by how little we understand our own language. More than just the language help is the invaluable experience of getting to know a person from another culture one-on-one. I wish every American could have such an experience, to share ideas and stories. Our world would not be in such turmoil if more people had these opportunities for understanding.[10]

Remember to celebrate their special days—birthdays, graduation day, and *their* national holidays. *You* are their family away from home! And you have intentionally built a bridge to their spiritual need!

INFLUENCING THEM SPIRITUALLY

Christian love goes beyond the material needs of people. We know the most important need is their spiritual need. Our Lord tried to meet this need while He healed and fed the multitudes. There are at least three important ways in which internationals become curious about the Christian faith. The first is through their taste of Christian love. This starts with meeting their felt needs. It is the most powerful way of demonstrating to them that God is love. Remember that other religions do not have the same concept of God. Our love builds the bridge of friendship not only between them and us, but also between them and God.

Along with love we should expose them to the Christian faith. This could be in very natural ways, such as praying before meals or inviting them to go to a Christian concert or movie with you. Make sure beforehand that the movie is truly Christian! Inviting them for a Bible study or forcing them to attend church before they are ready, which they may do out of the graciousness of their culture, may be counter-productive. Then adding the difficult language of "Christianese" to their struggle with English may be very frustrating.

The emphasis should be the life and teachings of Christ, not Christian culture. And, definitely not a criticism of their religion or that of others.

Witnessing on a one-to-one basis is often possible with internationals. This means sharing your personal experience with Christ, not explaining theology! You may get opportunities for it as they ask questions or as you discover areas in which they are struggling. You should not hide your faith from them nor apologize for it. They like stories so tell them the stories of God's significance in your life.

It is good to be aware of the basic beliefs of other religions, so you can be sensitive about the differences. For example, for Muslims the opportunity of forgiveness of sins here and now without having to wait for the Day of Judgment is something worth emphasizing. For Hindus, the opportunity to be liberated from the cycles of birth and death due to karma is an attractive aspect of the Christian faith. The concept of God being personal and loving is by far the most attractive discovery for the international. The fact that *He* provided the way of forgiveness of sin is mind-boggling to most internationals. Your *agape* love for them will reinforce this.

Let your life itself be a witness. Let the international see the difference in your life and relationships as a Christian. Your joy, peace, and love in your family speak loudly to the international as he spends time with you in your home. Your practical adherence to absolute Truth may initially frustrate him. But when he sees your persistent belief in absolutes, your friendship with an international has great potential. It can be the key to winning him for Christ. Yes, *you* could be that foreign missionary who reaches that international friend in the comfort of your own home. You could be the one that hears from the lips of our Lord on that glorious day: *"I was a stranger, and you took Me in"* (Matt 25:35).

I am so enthused about international student opportunities; we *must* listen to one more testimony:

GOD FOUND ME IN AMERICA
A testimony by Wichit Maneevone

Alone, under a tree on a campus in Pittsburgh, I pondered my plight. I had problems. It was hard to understand the language and customs of the people around me. When I tried to speak, no one had time to listen to my stumbling speech. I missed my family and friends. I did not enjoy eating the strange, bland food of Americans. Why was I here?

Back home in Thailand, I had done well in high school and at the university. My father said he would help support me while I studied abroad for my master's degree, which would bring me a better job and social prestige.

So I sold my land and bought a ticket to Pittsburgh where I had a Thai friend. On arriving, I found little of the glamour and fun portrayed in the movies of Hollywood. Instead, I found it to be a very lonely place. I had taken an intensive English course for four months, but I could not find anyone who would stop long enough to let me practice. That day, I longed to return to Thailand. I felt that nothing—not even saving face for myself and my family—could be worth the sadness and emptiness I was experiencing.

Just then an American, a total stranger, came and sat down by me. He not only talked with me, but he invited me to his home. Such a thing had never happened before. I was delighted to see the inside of an American home. Fred Wolfe and his wife asked about me, then about my family and they explained some of their customs. Someone cared!

Later I learned that they were Christians. Although I didn't care about their religion, I went to church with them because I wanted to practice my English, and because the people there were friendly and happy. I kept wondering why they were different.

Why did Mr. Wolfe care about me? I had nothing to give him. Yet I could call him whenever I needed help. When he told me that Jesus Christ had made him a different person, I had much to ponder.

Pittsburgh was too cold, so I moved to Los Angeles. Through International Students, Inc., I met more Christian families. They were very good to me. I began to see from their lives that I lacked something. The Reddings took me on special retreats and often had me in their home. They told me more about the Lord Jesus Christ. Rather than pressuring me, they let me have time to think things through for myself.

Under the impact of John 3:16 and John 14:6, I received Christ as my Savior. Almost immediately I wrote to my father and told him about my decision to believe in Jesus. He did not reply for several months. When I finally received his letter, he expressed bitter disappointment in me and said that I was no longer his son. Sadness would have overwhelmed me had it not been for my

Christian friends who helped me and showed great love and concern. They assured me that I now had a heavenly Father who loved me and wanted the best for me.

In Thailand there is a strict Buddhist custom that requires a son to serve time in the monastery to gain enough merit for his parents' salvation. Since I was the only son in the family, this duty fell to me. My father feared that there was now no hope of gaining a sufficient amount of merit to insure his salvation. He cut off all financial support, and I was left without income to pay for my rent, food, and school expenses. God provided, however, for my friends found a Christian American host family with whom I was able to live.

That year was not easy, but God enabled me to cope with my trying circumstances. I was no longer lonely, and all my needs were supplied by God's grace. Christians were kind and prayed for me. They were not the "hello, see you later" kind of people I encountered at school.

After I earned my master's degree and had worked in the States for a couple of years, I left for Thailand. I went with my American wife and child. I feared the hardships we would have to face. But the Lord was faithful to His Word and helped me as I met family and friends. To my great joy, they welcomed me back with greater love and warmth than they had ever shown before.

We had many opportunities to share God's love. My mother responded and accepted Jesus. To this day, she is the only Christian in her village. Although my father listened, he said he was not yet ready for such a decision. My best friend, a university professor, asked Jesus to come into his heart. Watcheree, my sister who had become a Christian while visiting me in the U.S., was maintaining her Christian witness in a nursing school, and was eager to help her classmates come to love Jesus.

How grateful I am that Christians in the United States helped me when I was lonely in a strange land. They taught me about Christ, not only by their words, but also by their love, kindness, and patience. They took me in when my own family disowned me. They encouraged me to grow in the knowledge of Jesus, until I was better able to stand by myself. They gave me a vision that I too can be involved in God's plan to reach, not only my own people, but also others from all over the world.

Now we are back in the United States on the International Students staff because we are concerned for the need to reach internationals on our campuses—those who will be future leaders. I spend my time befriending lonely students. What a privilege it is for me to tell them about Jesus Christ and to share His love with them![11]

Ministering Christ's love to international students is one of the finest ways to do world missions at home. There are so many levels of involvement for you. But the time commitment or relating to intellectuals may not be within your interest. So let's look at another group of internationals who live among us: Missionary Kids: Citizens of the World.

Missionary Kids:
3 Citizens Of The World

Susan was just graduating from high school. She had been voted number one in her class...of four. Emotions were running high. This was the big day! Her family was proudly smiling. Her friends were congratulating her. She had delivered the valedictorian speech flawlessly. It was a clear plaudit of the school and her family, and it was a dramatic challenge to the pursuit of excellence. Her cap and gown were as authentic as any.

Yet, strangely, there were distinct differences in this graduation ceremony. Her corsage was a brilliant cascade of twelve Cymbidium orchids, picked just this morning, chosen from the thousands of parasite clusters hanging from the banyan trees along the conya, a narrow waterway between a lake and river in the Amazon Rain Forest. There were only four graduates, and though Susan and her family and the other graduates and their families were a suntanned, Caucasian white, the majority of the guests were of golden brown skin. Her speech had to be translated into two languages other than the one in which she spoke. Susan herself had used those other languages on several occasions in her speech. The main speaker was the noble tribal chief of the Shiro Indians. Susan's dad had to interpret for him.

Yes, Susan is an MK (missionary kid)! Or, as some would say, a TCK (third culture kid). Though she retains some aspects of her parents' home cultures, she adds parts of the culture of her resident country, forming a third culture, for she was raised on the mission field. In fact, she was born there!

I was immediately confronted by this third culture phenomenon when I went to teach junior high MKs. They were shouting, "Viva! Peru! Viva! Peru!" with innuendoes of "Down with America!" I said, "Let's walk one-half kilometer off this "Little America" center, draw water from the muddy river, share an outhouse with several other families, sleep in a hammock hung over a dirt floor after blowing out your candle (your only source of light), watch your little sister die of pneumonia because your parents don't have the money to take her to the hospital, and hope that you get at least a third-grade education before having to go to the fields to work. And then, shout, "Long live Peru!" They were living in all the beauty and security of the virgin Amazon Rain Forest, but enjoying the comforts of America.

Nineteen years ago, Susan's young parents had made a career commitment to the mission agency. In their first year on the field, Susan was born. All the joys of parenting were theirs. Only, instead of a choice of gender/specific absorbent, non-allergenic disposable diapers, the cloth ones did just fine. Instead of concerns over cat-hair allergies, they struggled with hepatitis contracted from her pet monkey. Instead of teen dating problems, they consoled their teenager because the two boys her age, she knew like "brothers." Instead of the "full closet—'I've got nothing to wear'!" scenario, they had a hard time getting her out of her favorite cushma, a sack-like, coarse-woven Shiro dress.

Lest you get the wrong impression and begin thinking I am describing a mal-developed youth, read on:

Susan grew up swimming like a fish, climbing trees like a monkey, running the jungle paths like a panther. She knew how to work like a horse, sing like a bird, and play like a puppy. She was fit as a fiddle, her family was as tight as a drum, and she had no need to go around tooting her own horn!

Did I say that she ranked in the top percentile in her SAT scores? That several colleges offered her academic scholarships? That she was fluent in two languages and conversant in a third, the Shiro dialect, into which her dad was translating the New Testament?

Oh, yes! Susan was no fish out of water! In Peru, that is! But for three years of her life, she had to leave "home" and return to the homelands of her parents. You see, her mother is Canadian, her dad, a U.S. citizen. Because she was born in Peru, Susan was also able to claim that nation's citizenship...until she was eighteen.

Faced with the dilemma of relinquishing one of them, she turned to me for counsel. "I don't believe I will ever want to live in Canada. But how do I not offend my mother if I deny my Canadian citizenship? I think I should keep my American passport. But I also want to remain in *my* country, Peru! I am Peruvian, aren't I? I was born here. It is very likely I will want to return here after my college studies."

As I was saying, when Susan was four years old, she joined her dad and mom (and baby brother) on a one-year furlough. Darting from city to city and church to church, she learned little of her Canadian or American culture and heritage. For six months they did stay put in a country village in Georgia with Grandma and Grandpa, while Mom and Dad continued to travel. That was good. It gave some stability to her life.

Again, when Susan was nine, they ventured "home" for a furlough. Much of the same, except this time the children stayed in Canada with their mom's folks.

At 14, though, Susan had quite another experience! She had been attending a K-12 grade mission school with a total of 34 students. Now, in the States again, she entered a four-year high school with 1500 students! Here is an excerpt from a story she wrote upon her return to Peru:

The sun shone gaily that terrifying morning. Slowly Tom and I trudged out to the road. Through my mind raced a thousand questions: Where am I going? What should I do? How will I feel? As I looked toward the woods, memories of my favorite tree in Peru came back to me. If I were in that tree, I wouldn't have to worry about this dreaded day. I would know everybody. Why? Why? Oh! Why did this have to happen to me?

Then I saw it—that bright orange bus. My heart started thumping. Each beat came a little faster. That rattling, rusting behemoth came like a tremendous comber to drown me in a tidal wave of faces without meaning. Unwillingly I stepped into the bus and sat down next to Tom. These kids all knew each other, but what about me? On my right was Tom, but his face was expressionless. (He would attend an adjacent middle school.) I found no refuge in him from this giant chamber of faces, all yelling and screaming their own delight on this first day of school.

How unlike the usual calm stroll I used to know walking to school...just the birds singing and an occasional comment from a neighboring house. How this was so different, changed completely in this squeaky, cranky old bus. At every stop the noise would rise until it was like a buzz of a huge bee close to my ear. But I could not shoo it away.

In what seemed like minutes I could see the town ahead, drawing closer—every moment pulling me into a world of unknowns. I didn't know what to expect. I saw other buses like our own as we drove onward. Then there it was, looming ahead of us, its windows flashing the reflection of the early sun. We circled the monstrous wood and brick building and came to a stop.

> Like a bottle of water poured out, we left the bus. We surged forward, carried irresistibly towards the building's mouth and momentarily I stopped at its gapping doors. I turned to get one last glimpse of the bus as it departed. The orange mass of metal, which had so recently been the object of my despair, now seemed like the only hope I had of getting back home.
>
> It was gone. I was now in the monster's throat! I felt a downward, sinking feeling. I was being swallowed alive![1]

But Susan's life in the jungle had made her resilient. And she came through that year a stronger and wiser young lady.

And now it was graduation day. The orchids were beautiful. The party was a gala affair, blending the cultures and hearts of many people into one as they bid yet another farewell to Susan.

Furlough for her folks was another year away. They could have taken an early one to help Susan get adjusted. But as a family they had come to a decision. They reasoned together: Dad was close to completing the first draft of the Shiro New Testament. Valuable editing help was available now. A good college had been chosen. She would live in the dorm. Mary, a friend who had graduated from this mission school two years earlier was a Junior at the college Susan had chosen to attend.

It was decided. Susan would return to the States— alone! She is now an adult, they say—an American adult! Citizenship of her dad's country (with her Peruvian passport) is the one she chose to keep. But her culture is a sweet blend of at least four. Truly, Susan is an international who lives among us. She will probably be in your church this Sunday. It is possible that she has even been in your church for many years already.[2]

An Adult Missionary Kid (AMK) may have joined your church without announcing his background. He may have grown up in a little African village, hiding in the middle of the Congo jungle. Or in the cultural center of Paris where he learned first hand about arts, literature and dance. Or in the continually buzzing metropolis of Hong Kong with its millions of people. These children of missionaries grew up with broadening experiences. At an early age they were confronted with various lifestyles in a country and culture that are foreign to their parents' upbringing. At five they held by the tail a (dead) Mamba snake and called for their mother to take a picture to send home to Grandma. At six they climbed the thirty-foot water tower. At sixteen they were considering relationships with the local youth. After all, though their parents see the cultural differences, having been raised there, these youth feel as much a part of the local culture as do the nationals. Most, though, forego developing that relationship to return to their parents' home culture for their college education.

And they are in your church. They may have typical jobs in your neighborhood: a plumber; a music teacher; a doctor or a homemaker. But they have a wealth of experience and knowledge of a world bigger than your community. Unfortunately, that resource too often remains latent and unutilized. At a time when your church is becoming more active in intercultural affairs (yet acknowledging a dearth of inter-culturally competent persons), you might find AMKs to be "link-people" who can be an important resource for a world of understanding and play a role as mediator on the world scene of human relations.

But to minister to this group of internationals and help them to develop to their potential, certain deliberate action steps should be taken. The following are a dozen or more ideas for you to consider.

ACTION STEP ONE: DISCARD MYTHS ABOUT MKS

The American church as a whole suffers under the delusion of several myths about MKs that places them as distinctly different from the broader population of youth. Discard these myths about MKs and help others in your fellowship discard them, also.

Myth #1: There is a certain amount of deprivation and personality underdevelopment resulting from a missionary overseas upbringing.

MKs are not disadvantaged as many suppose, but are more likely a normal, well-adjusted and privileged group of young people. MKs, as members of a third culture, are in many ways advantaged far above their American counterparts. They have been exposed to an extended world perspective, developed cross-cultural skills and acquired languages and the ability to relate comfortably with nationals as peers. As a result of their experiences, many are familiar with poverty and hunger. They have a broader and more sober outlook on the world than many Christian youth in the United States. They have developed a "second set of eyes" through which they can process life's issues.

Most are highly intelligent, emotionally stable, conscientious, conservative, relaxed, honest. Some have emotional problems but the rate is not greater than among the general American population. The cross-cultural international exposure provides for a personality depth beyond the level of the average American youth.

Some may tend to be more reserved—to withdraw somewhat in new situations, but there is not a significant deprivation factor built into their overall experience. MKs, in general, have fewer psychological problems than youth from similar age groups in the USA.

Our oldest son graduated first in his class of...one! (He graduated mid-year.) He stayed on in Brazil for another year. Because of his fluency in Portuguese, he accepted a responsible position with the mission. But he went home a year before we did to attend college.

Prior to his two-year experience in Brazil, he had enjoyed life in the jungles of Peru. As a young teenager he had exhibited his entrepreneurial prowess by raising chickens and selling them to families on the Mission Center. He had also spent 18 days in a dugout canoe, paddling up the Ucayali River to where it joined the Amazon River, accompanying Jim, who had won a national Canadian bicycle race. His government had commissioned him to bicycle to the capitals in the Western Hemisphere, carrying a Parchment of Unity to the Ministers of Education. Their signature would affirm their agreement to raise the standard of education among all children.

As I was saying, he came home before us to attend college. In relating with other students, stories of where they had been, what they had done regularly came up. One young lady's story in particular shocked him so much that he sent us a message on a cassette tape. Better than he could have in written form, he verbally expressed his utter surprise and disbelief that until this girl had come to college, she had not ventured more than thirty miles from where she had been born! If cultural deprivation was to be known, he had found it in her story!

Myth #2: MKs suffer academically.

There is no evidence for a generalization such as this. On the contrary, the average IQ score of an MK runs between 15 and 20 points above the general population of the USA. It has also been determined that MKs are the brightest academic achievers among all TCK groupings (Third Culture Kids—children of diplomats, multi-national corporations, humanitarian organizations), maintaining a sterling record of academic achievement.

MKs take their academic achievement seriously and are frequently over-achievers. The daughter of some friends of ours began life as a bi-lingual, learning English from her father and a Filipino dialect from her mother. She began her formal education at three years old. Mandarin Chinese is the required language in Hong Kong schools but Cantonese is still the spoken language of the street. At age five she entered Primary School speaking, reading and writing three languages, and speaking a fourth!

MKs do a great deal of reading and are more likely to enjoy writing than their peers in the USA. TCKs, in general, are giving a higher intellectual performance at the same time that the general scores in the USA are going down. On the Standard Achievement Test (SAT), these students are ranking 14.5 months above the USA national average. On college-board entrance exams, TCK graduates are ranking 20-24 percentile points above the national average.

With the wide use of home schooling on the mission fields, and its advantages, universities are recruiting home-schooled youth, knowing their achievement exceeds that of mass classroom teaching. Research indicates that homeschooled students typically do very well in college, not just academically, but socially as well. Skills learned in homeschooling translate very well to the college campus, with strong self-discipline and motivation. Colleges recognize this advantage, including Brown University representative Joyce Reed, who shares, "These kids are the epitome of Brown students." She believes they make a good fit with the university because "they've learned to be self-directed, they take risks, they face challenges with total fervor, and they don't back off."[3]

MKs suffer academically? It's just not true! In fact, the single group that has the largest number of individuals listed in the Who's Who in America is MKs! (Note: Statistics change more rapidly than fashions! A

Google search will help you with current stats on these points.)

Myth #3: MKs are rebellious toward their parents and the Christian faith.

Generally, MKs are more intimately related to and dependent on the family than would be true in the U.S. Missionary parents play a vital role in the socialization of their children. Beyond the immediate family (unless they are in a very isolated ministry location), children of missionaries have a host of "aunts and uncles"—other members of the missions community to help reinforce the Biblical principles of healthy living.

It is true, however, if the rules of Christian conduct have only been imposed on the youth and not formed deeply into his fabric of life, entering his "home" U.S. culture could be traumatic. Rules and parents and aunts and uncles have a way of deciding for you. Without those structures to guide him, the MK will have to decide for himself whether or not he will retain the moral values his parents taught him. Stateside teens, of course, face the same issues but usually have more opportunity— and at an earlier age—to work out their own feelings than the MK who has lived with strict guidelines until he is suddenly thrust into the freedom of adulthood. In his favor, however, is the fact that he is more mature when he has to make those independent choices. MKs are vulnerable, open, tolerant. They need guidance of a special type; not overpowering, but a "standing in the wings" to be there if they "miss their lines" on this new stage of life. Will you be there for them when they come home?

Myth #4: Boarding homes are basically detrimental to a child's development and serve to lower his self-concept.

Extensive studies have been conducted in light of this myth. Conclusion after conclusion documents that

MKs in boarding schools develop personalities very much like those of non-boarders. In one study, out of thirty-two personality traits, MK boarders differed from day students only in one trait, and that just slightly. Boarding students seemed a bit restrained while the non-boarders were slightly adventurous.

A far greater factor in a child's self-concept, whether as a boarding or non-boarding student, is the attitude of the parents. "You mean, God called *us* to be missionaries!" The five year old danced happily around her parents when told that God had placed a new call on their *family*. But it didn't begin when the girl was five. Her parents already had been giving their daughter a broader worldview.

Myth #5: Because the MKs' parents are busy serving the Lord full time, the Lord makes up for the gaps in the children's upbringing.

Closely related to the previous myth, this misunderstanding harbors a parent's delinquency in fulfilling their role as parents in a cross-cultural ministry setting. No matter what cultural setting, parents are still parents, and have the primary responsibility for their children's growth and development.

Tragedy lies in the path of parents who communicate verbally (or more often, non-verbally) that their children are in the way of their "work for the Lord." It was my unfortunate experience to deal with one such family, and the results, years later, left both adult children in the cauldrons of worldly dissipation!

Myth #6: MKs really don't have any problems to worry about.

All of this is not to say that MKs do not have needs and problems. MKs are kids...like all kids that we know. The temptations of this world and the transition to adulthood, with the added adjustment between two or even three cultures can bring heartache, discouragement and failure. Most of the needs and potential problems for MKs are in the area of social adjustment when they return to North America after years in another culture.

Yet, some apparently "silly little thing" could also yield frustration. Susan, remember, was a summa cum laude graduate and valedictorian speaker. Yet, when she walked across the Los Angeles airport terminal to a drinking fountain and could not figure out how to turn it on, you can only imagine her frustration.

MKs will not want to talk about such things. *You* need to develop a sixth sense to know when something is bothering the one you have decided to help adjust to their new "home" culture.

Action Step One has taken some time to state and illustrate, but these myths must be dispelled to move forward in meaningful care for adult MKs. If you try to approach an MK while harboring any one of the above myths, your offer of help will likely be shunned.[4]

ACTION STEP TWO: BECOME INFORMED

By reading this chapter on ministering to MKs who are living among us, you have begun taking this step. Though Susan is a fictitious person, everything I wrote about her is from my personal experience of working with missionary kids. But as the Christian community in America is more and more realizing the needs of these internationals, more articles and books are becoming available. Look for them. Read them. Become informed. A 0.21 second Google search of "missionary kids" identified "about 87,000" results. A 0.19 second Google search of "Third Culture Kids" yielded "about 180,000" results. Or, you could spend days on YouTube, listening to MKs tell their stories of success or failure, of their joys and fears. Become informed!

ACTION STEP THREE: DISCOVER YOUR MKS

Listen to this father describe one aspect of the kind of background you will discover your MKs have:

> Good to hear from you. But we don't live in Texas anymore. We have just returned to our home in Singapore from Finland and Sweden. We have lived in Singapore for the last 4 years. I am on the Senior Leadership team of the (mission agency). We were in Finland for the 40th anniversary of the (mission agency) and stopped by Sweden to meet our son's future in-laws as his fiancée is from Gothenburg, Sweden. They were missionaries to Tunisia and Saudi Arabia; her mother is from Norway, her father from Sweden. Alice, his fiancée, has lived more outside of Sweden than in it. So our son who was born in Indonesia, who has lived in several different countries and States in the USA, is marrying Alice in Hawaii where all three of our boys now live.

That is how global our world has become!

Find out how many MKs whose parents are supported by your church are currently in college. What are their names? What college are they attending? What are their needs? Their parents could probably help with much of this information. If they are in another city, is there a sister church near that college?

What about those who came home but didn't go on to college? Who are they? Where are they? What are they doing? Because you are serious about this ministry opportunity, you are going to leave "no stone unturned" in discovering these details.

If your fellowship is not the sending church for any missionaries with returning MKs, identify other MKs who may be attending your fellowship, who are enrolled in a local college or working in your neighborhood. This might take some sleuthing! Those who are not having a good experience in their new home culture could have their feelings buried quite deeply.

Further, discover your Adult Missionary Kids (AMK)— those who have been home for a long time. Many, too many, have not had the pleasure of a good reentry experience or adjustment to American life.

I was doing a reentry seminar for a church just ready to send out their first missionary family. They had followed the principles of the book, *Serving As Senders~Today*, and wanted to be prepared for the family's return. Following that meeting, one lady approached me, sobbing uncontrollably. Through tears, she cried, "All I wanted to do was to go back! All I wanted to do was to go back!" She had been raised on the mission field. When she turned eighteen, the family had come home. Her reentry care consisted of her father saying, "You are living in America now; just live like an American." For twenty years she had thought: "All I want to do is to go back!" She is married with three children. "All I wanted to do was to go back," she sobbed! I cried with her. After many tears and gentle rapport-building, I said, "Mary, you are fortunate that you never had the opportunity to go back." Her surprised expression encouraged me to give the reason: "The dream of your childhood that you have built up in your mind was probably never true, and for sure, it is not a reality there now. If you had gone back, your disappointment in a dream proven untrue could have totally devastated you." She thanked me for the steps to a good reentry that I had shared in the seminar. "I can now begin my reentry," she concluded.

On another occasion, a gentleman met me after I had just conducted a seminar on reentry. Holding back a river of tears, he admitted that though he had been home from the field for over ten years, there were so many unresolved issues still stirring in his soul. He had not yet found anyone who would listen to his expressions of need.

I have not conducted a single seminar on reentry without at least one person coming to me, crying out their story for help. The most recent was a Vietnamese domestic worker who had just returned from a year in Malaysia. She said she represented 30 workers who were all having trouble on their reentry to Vietnam.

Discover the MKs who are living among you!

ACTION STEP FOUR: LAY A STRATEGY

You, and a group from your congregation with whom you have been sharing these new opportunities of ministry, are becoming excited and want to get involved. Excitement can often get us involved in projects that we are not able to handle. Lay a strategy on ideas that you can follow through. These ideas, often so new to a congregation's thinking, require clear, realistic planning. Consider with how many MKs and with which ones your fellowship is able to minister? Possibly certain general needs of a larger group of MKs could be met, while more time/finance intensive needs of a smaller group could be handled. For example, kindness with a birthday card could be shown to every MK that you contacted, whereas college financial assistance possibly could be afforded for only one or two.

ACTION STEP FIVE: DEVELOP A PEOPLE RESOURCE LIST

Even at this initial stage of offering help to returning MKs, plan to enlist many different people. One person cannot do it all! Begin a list of people in the church who are willing to offer their services to the MKs you select to help: An accountant to help with taxes and budget, a mechanic willing to give advice on a car purchase or maintenance, a doctor, dentist, optometrist who will give the care needed, a lawyer to help with legal matters, a friend who will listen when the MK needs to talk! Families whose homes are "always open."

ACTION STEP SIX: FOCUS ON THE SOCIAL/EMOTIONAL NEEDS

Communicate with them often—by whatever media is available in today's world! Occasionally, call them, perhaps on their birthday. Because they are particularly vulnerable at holiday time, make sure they have a place to go and someone to be with during these times. Initiate these steps. Don't expect them to ask...they won't!

Knowing in advance that an MK will be attending a college in your town or returning for some secular or ministry position, arrange for them to spend the summer between their high school junior and senior year with you. It could give them work experience, an opportunity to obtain their driver's license, open a bank account, begin their Stateside transition, still within the guidelines of your Godly home. Become their mentor/confidant to help ease the strain of multiple adjustments after graduation.

ACTION STEP SEVEN: HELP MEET FINANCIAL NEEDS

Provide your own scholarship plan to assist with college bills. Pay for one semester or one class. Ask the college to match your gift. Provide funds for certain hours of internship with the church. Student debt is the single greatest deterrent to a graduate entering a life of ministry. And the double-digit percentages of increase in tuition—particularly in Bible colleges—over the past decade, doesn't make this picture look much brighter. Rather than Susan having to buy a computer, could she use the church's in the late afternoon? Or that "extra" one you have in the den? Instead of her having to purchase an extensive library of textbooks, could you help her search the Internet for inexpensive used texts. Or, are there recent graduates of that college in your fellowship who could loan or give her theirs?

ACTION STEP EIGHT: HELP MKS SECURE A JOB

When Susan arrived in your town, though a scholarship paid for her tuition, she had living expenses to meet. She wanted and needed a job, but she found it difficult since she had never before had a paying job. Show her how to write a résumé. Teach her how to complete an application. Help her practice presenting herself in an in-person, telephone or Skype interview.

ACTION STEP NINE: HELP MKS BECOME MOBILE

Susan found her bicycle to be adequate for her time in Peru, that is, until someone brought a Honda 70 to the mission center. Then, "everybody" needed to move up a notch in their means of transportation. But, buy a car? It was never a thought. She needs help in choosing a car... selecting good insurance... managing a driver's education course... getting her driver's license. Maybe she even needs to learn how to drive! A bit overwhelming for her? Unless you are there to help! Will you let her use your car to practice her driving?

ACTION STEP TEN: HELP MKS WITH BUDGETING

Susan certainly knows the value of money. How many months did Dad have them "tighten their belts" because funds didn't arrive from their partnership team? Or, more often, they gave to those who were truly poor, thus limiting funds for themselves. But what international calling card is the best for her to use to call her Mom when she is particularly homesick? Can you help her reason whether or not she needs that "newest and nicest" item that she has never had and finds hard to resist? Can you maneuver the often-treacherous details of income tax filing? Help her with hers? Help her compare prices on the Internet instead of running from store to store. Does she realize that buying something for twice the price if the item is guaranteed to last four times as long is a better investment of her funds? What about a bank account? Checks? Does she know how to write one? Credit cards? Does she know the dangers of overspending with "plastic" money? Yet, the convenience of a card, *if* she can control her spending? Has she had established deep in her consciousness the importance of tithing or the "hilarious" giving of II Corinthians 8:14? Does she know the "willing mind" principle of II Corinthians 8:12?[5]

ACTION STEP ELEVEN: HELP MKS SORT THROUGH THEIR CLOSET OF CLOTHES

Susan grew up where clothes were more functional than fashionable. Remember her cushma!—that sack-like, coarse-woven Shiro dress? No, it is not necessary (or good) to transform her into a fashion model with every fad swing in styles. But it is important that Christians do not draw undue attention to themselves by either funky or fad clothing. Susan would more than appreciate a woman taking her shopping occasionally. The guys would especially appreciate the practical assistance of someone in your fellowship who would actually enjoy washing and ironing and mending their clothes!

ACTION STEP TWELVE: OPEN YOUR HOME

Open your home to all of the MKs in your fellowship and neighboring colleges. There is nothing that compares to the home atmosphere to help MKs make the transitional adjustments to the "back home" of America. Invite them often for a meal, an evening of family games, or ask them to join you on family outings. But don't just issue a general invitation, such as "Come over any time you like." Rather, call with a specific idea: "We're having a popcorn auction tonight. Bring an item—any silly thing you would want to get rid of. Popcorn will be our money." If that is too crazy of an idea, invite them to a more calm game night or movie night or craft night or a swim in your pool followed with a barbeque. Such a specific invitation will let them know that you really do want them to be involved in your family activities.

Open your home for all the MK students of a particular year (or years) of a certain mission location or missionary school to enjoy a holiday reunion.

Open your home for college MK students to live with you for free or for minimal cost for the summer break, allowing them to save money for the next year's tuition. Or, have them live with you for a semester, or a year.

Open your home for a real home-cooked Sunday dinner. If Susan (or Bill) likes to cook, take them shopping, buy the ingredients and let them cook in your kitchen. Let them treat you to the exotic dishes of the jungle or metropolis that was their home. Or teach them to bake pies or bread, or cook American foods that they may not know how to cook.

Open your home to let them do their laundry!

Open your home and your heart. Become the "aunt and uncle" or "grandmother and granddad" that they can confide in.

Open your home!

ACTION STEP THIRTEEN: PREPARE FOR THEIR ARRIVAL

Do some research on the country from which they are coming. Know the ministry in which their parents (and possibly they) have been involved. Learn as much as you can of their interests, their abilities, their talents, their fears and anxieties. Have a welcoming party on their arrival...on the correct date and flight schedule! Yes, it happened. The church family showed up a day late. Fortunately, his parents were there to meet him on time. Post their pictures in the church foyer for several weeks in advance so when they arrive people don't ask if they are just visiting. Place an insert in the bulletin giving good reentry questions to ask. Definitely not: "How was your trip?" Or, "I'll bet you are really glad to be home now."

Here is a handful of suggestions. Let them spur your own creativity:

- What or who did you have to leave behind that you think you will really miss?
- Have you faced any major surprises since being here?
- What is the funniest thing that you remember about your last time here?
- What do you think will be the most intimidating/ challenging aspect of your adjustment here?
- In what way can we be of most help to you? If they don't have any ideas, suggest some ways in which you have prepared yourself to help.

But, four years later, when they are graduating from college, don't stop caring for them. The first year out of college is particularly rough for MKs. It is another "real world" adjustment, and that again without their parents' guidance.

Dear reader, I trust by now your heart and mind have been challenged to the needs of the MKs who live among us. Are you excited? I trust I have filled your mind with ideas! And as your own creativity has been stirred, I am sure you have thought of additional ways to extend helpful friendship to the "Susans" in your fellowship. However, these next two Action Steps are by far the most critical ministry you can offer your MK!

ACTION STEP FOURTEEN: HELP MKS SORT THROUGH THEIR VALUE SYSTEM

(Stated in dispelling Myth#3 above, but included here for emphasis.) Susan must now decide for herself if she will retain the moral, ethical and spiritual values her parents taught her. Stateside teens face the same issues but have more opportunity to work out their feelings at a younger age than the MK who has lived within the strict guidelines all her life. And the mission community life has provided a host of "aunts and uncles" to support her parents' teachings. The rules of center life have been clearly defined for her.

A definite positive to this matter is this: Because most MKs are more mature when they have to confront their parents' standards, they will act more responsibly in those choices as they are provided a safe environment in your counsel. Your credibility for this mentoring level of relationship will come as you spend time with her through the aforementioned activities.

(We have used "Susan" as an example in many of these Action Steps. It goes without saying that for the young men in your fellowship, a man will fulfill most of these opportunities to minister.)

ACTION STEP FIFTEEN: PRAY FOR YOUR MKS

Because Susan's family has been actively engaged in taking enemy territory, they have no doubt been the target of heavy spiritual attack. Even though Susan is now geographically removed from them, she will continue to be satan's object of assault. Any signs of failure on the part of their daughter will, at the least, distract her parents from their mission work and at the greatest, will bring one or both parents home from the field.

Prayer is one of the two main weapons in spiritual warfare. Take full advantage of fervent prayer for the MKs living among us.[6,7]

AN MK DECLARATION

A group of MKs wanted us to have a better understanding of them. Thus, they wrote a formal MK Declaration:

We, a body of MKs, in order to form a more correct conception of ourselves, establish truth, promote understanding, and secure the blessings of cultural identity for ourselves and our posterity, do ordain and establish this *Declaration Against Stereotypical Conceptions* on behalf of the MKs of the world.

We hold these truths to be self-evident:

§   That America is not the only wonderful place in the world to live. For we have learned, in whatever nation we are, there to be content—if not downright happy.

§   That growing up in America does not guarantee satisfactory emotional adjustment. And that growing up in a country other than the U.S. does not imply maladjustment, contrary to the theories of some professors of MK psychology.

§   That MKs as a class are not in need of therapy or counseling before they are able to take their places as valid and valuable members of society. Rather than being poorly adjusted, MKs in general are many times more likely to be found on dean's lists and in leadership positions of all kinds other than in therapy groups.

§   That those MKs who do have problems adjusting or feeling unhappy in America are not to be criticized. They probably represent a small minority among American MKs. But we would also like to point out the millions of ordinary Americans who are in need of counseling or other assistance in adjustment. We suggest that adjustment is a human problem, not exclusively an MK one.

§   That there are worse fates than being 10,000 miles away from our parents. One of these might be growing up in a home where the parents are emotionally 10,000 miles away from each other, or from us. Furthermore, we suggest that homesickness is relative, upon observation of dozens of American college students who go home every weekend and still get homesick.

§   That, while it is advisable that we learn to relate comfortably to the nationals of America, as anywhere, it is also important that we preserve our own identities, standards and priorities. We maintain that we are not required to adjust too fully to a society, which does not adjust to meet the needs of its most helpless members.

§   That being atypical or individualistic or even un-American is not equivalent to being poorly adjusted emotionally.

§   That MKs have a right to be different, and that within the broad group of MKs exists plenty of room for variation. For instance, some MKs are very homesick; others not at all. Some MKs are fluent in a second or third language; others much less so. Some consider themselves 90 percent the product of one culture and 10 percent of another. Some classify themselves as 40/60 percent either way. The one thing that can be stated for certain is, MKs are unique!

We hold that all Americans, non-Americans, and MKs are created equal; that they are endowed by their Creator with certain inalienable rights: that these are Life, Liberty and the pursuit of Cultural Identity.[8]

What a statement! Clearly spoken from their perspective. For even further understanding on the life of returning MKs, written in their words, read Chapter Eight of the book, *The Reentry Team.*[9,10]

Reentry to one's home culture is often the most difficult time of the overseas experience. In this chapter we have talked about youth who are entering the culture of their parents—a culture barely familiar to them. MKs, citizens of the world, will be grateful when you extend a helping hand to them during this transition. And their parents—what peace of mind! And their work on the field will progress better with the calm assurance that all is well at home.

This may be your calling. If so, pursue it with all speed. On the other hand, you may find the challenge of those who are in our country illegally more suited to your personality. In the next chapter, we will survey this opportunity.

4 ILLEGAL ALIENS

Illegal aliens: This is a cold, hard term to place on a human being created in the image of God, wooed by the Holy Spirit to worship and honor Him, and destined to spend eternity either in His presence or forever forbidden entrance. It is a hard term: Illegal alien.

In deference to the conscience of the world, any number of euphemisms have been coined to soften the harsh sound of that term. "Undocumented guest" seems to be the most kind—at the moment, at least. But name them what you will, they represent the segment of our population with the most dramatic growth. And they pose some of the most difficult issues in our society.

Stereotypically, we peer into a smoke-filled room. There is a lot of noise and disjointed commotion. We see a t-shirted potbelly with dangling legs, balancing on a spring-exposed couch. One arm is for bringing the hand to the mouth with the next can of beer; the other is for bringing a cigarette to the mouth for a final drag. The head is lost in a world of television make-believe that the mind does not fully comprehend. Monotonous boredom is punctuated by birth and life and death—possibly marriage, but not necessarily. Eating and sleeping and possibly working, but not necessarily.

Thus is life played out in the ghettos of unregistered aliens. In too many of them, anyway.

Until....

GOD'S LOVE COMES TO STRAWBERRY STREET
Like giant tectonic plates, two cultures meet on

Strawberry Street. The pressure builds. The differences rub and grate. And then, in demonstrated Christian love, they crush and crumble and produce the fertile soil for planting the Seed of God's Word in receptive hearts.

I was privileged to conduct the following telephone interview with Judy, Assistant Director of Strawberry Street Ministry. I have intentionally left it pretty much unedited—exposing, as she did, the grim realities of a tough ministry. I chose to do this because too many descriptions of ministry today are sugar-coated to appeal to our culture's quest for "Are we having fun yet?" In case you miss it in the interview, I will say it up front: A huge commendation to the people involved in this ministry is their faithful, consistent, persistent commitment to it!

Neal Pirolo: Judy, I was told that you are active in the ministry of your church to unregistered aliens.

Judy: Yes, I am. We are a bit discouraged right now. We are not seeing a lot of spiritual fruit.

NP: Oh! I'm sorry. Please tell me about it.

Judy: We are mostly inhibited by the language barrier. We currently have only one bi-lingual worker. The rest of us just sorta' make it through. When Rose Martinez, an orphanage director in Thailand, was here several months ago, she stayed with me. She said being able to live with the people and experience their culture is vital to reaching them. It is important for our workers to speak their language.

NP: How long have you been involved with these people?

Judy: The ministry started about 10 years ago. I have been with it for about the last five. It seems like we are

able to work best with the children. The young ones.
Until they are about age 14. Then they just drop out and
return to the ways so familiar to them. They drop out of
school. Get pregnant. Shift with the gangs.

NP: How do you deal with that?

Judy: Shortly after I got started in the ministry, we
decided to pull the 12-year-olds out of the group
activities of the younger ones and work with them on a
one-on-one basis. We bring them to our homes. Teach
them the basics—hygiene, cleaning, sewing, cooking.
Just teaching them how to read labels on cans, how to
prepare food that comes in boxes, how to live with the
things available to them in this society.

And, of course, all along the way we combine our
practical training with Bible studies and Scripture
memory. Those 12-year-olds are now 16. All five are still
in school and none are pregnant.

NP: Judy, that sounds to me like a major accomplishment!
I don't know where all this conversation is going to go, but
let me say at this point: From my perspective of working
with lots of different churches, and so many of them
launching bravely into various programs, I can only say
that the very fact that your church has stuck with these
people—in good times and bad—is commendable! Your
continued commitment to them has to be demonstrating
the everlasting love of God.

Judy: Well, thank you. But it is now with these girls
that we are at a crisis point. Just a few weeks ago in
a home Bible study situation, they were blatantly
disrespectful. There seems to be a real struggle with
interest and personal discipline. Two have called asking
for forgiveness but the other three are still holding out.

NP: Well, are you going to quit on them?

Judy: No! Of course not!

NP: That's my point. Good times and bad—you are there for them.

Judy: But this situation has given us a time for evaluation: Are we accomplishing what we want to accomplish? In their home life, we are making a big impact. They are better off. Their homes are clean and their personal hygiene is greatly improved.

We tried the Awana program, but they did not seem to respond positively to this. Sometimes when we help them with their Scripture memory it seems like we are only coaching them to repeat syllables—like they do not seem to understand the concepts.

NP: Are they not learning English in school?

Judy: The public schools are overwhelmed. They are trying but they end up just passing them on to the next grade. I met with the teacher of one of our 4th grade girls, Maria. The teacher had to look at her records to be sure which of her overcrowded class of children was Maria!

Maria's mother is one of eleven children. Four of her brothers and sisters were born here, but she is not yet a citizen. At age 25 she still does not speak English. In the home, Maria spoke nothing but Spanish until she was five. Then in kindergarten when she was to begin learning how to *read* English, she was just learning how to speak the language—and that without the support of the home environment.

Maybe five percent adapt. Another 20-25% hover at "D" level. The rest are totally falling between the cracks of two languages and cultures. They hang in until high school, and then drop out.

NP: That must have really hurt. Does your ministry provide any help in this area?

Judy: Oh, yes! We have developed a program of one-on-one tutoring to help them.

NP: There you go again. Maybe this conversation is a part of your evaluation to see just how much you *are* doing to help these people. That's great!

Judy: But there are so many who need help. Uriel is a freshman. He can't read. He survives by getting lost in the crowd. He plays it "low-key" so nobody will notice him. Next year, if he doesn't drop out, he will be a sophomore.

NP: Do you have a counterpart one-on-one program for your older boys?

Judy: Oh, yes. Uriel is an example. We have coupled him with a family. They gave him odd jobs every Saturday—all summer. Cleaning the pool, mowing the lawn—a little money and responsibility. He loved the attention, even to the point of saying, "I need help in school." They replied, "If you come to our house, we will help you." He started out, but when it got to the hard work of applying himself, he dropped out. Now, he's just "hiding in the crowd." We don't know if he will come around. It's easier to hang out. Few are motivated—most just get by as their parents get by.

Another thing: Though we may look on it as an undisciplined life style, it is probably just their cultural pattern—timing means nothing. For example, their teeth are really bad. Infants are given coke in their bottles to drink! Even before they lose their baby teeth, they are badly rotted. So we have a program to get them to the dentist every six months. We try to get them to do it themselves since we don't want to be just another welfare system—but we help. We can make it real clear that we will come to the house to pick them up at 3:00 pm for a dentist appointment, but if they decided at 2:45 to go to the flea market, they just wouldn't be there.

NP: Proverbs 31:9 makes it real clear that we are to *"plead the cause of the poor and needy"* but it also says we must *"judge righteously."* It must be difficult to make "righteous judgments."

Judy: We pray a lot. When we see a family that already doesn't have enough to live on, spending one third of their income on beer and cigarettes, do we put shoes on their kids' feet, or tell them to go buy shoes themselves? For some we do the former, others the latter. We deal with it just one situation at a time. Pepe, a 6th grader, let us know he wanted to be in the band—to play trumpet! Would we please get him a horn? He had located one in a pawnshop and we considered buying it. We would make a contract, loaning it to him as long as he was active in the band.

But then we found out that the school had instruments to loan. So, on our recommendation, they let him use one. It takes a lot of legwork to find out what benefits they are eligible for.

Jesse, a fellow from our body, took Pepe to one of the Celebrant Singers concerts, in which he played the trumpet. After Jesse settles into his Community College work, he has agreed to tutor Pepe.

Any opportunity we have to couple our kids one-on-one with someone who will give them time, we'll do it. We are not trying to destroy their culture—just help them learn how to live in their dual culture. And, of course, we want to expose them to the Word of God through Bible studies and Scripture memory. His Word will not return void.

When we take them swimming on Fridays, their "ticket" to go is to have a new verse memorized. But they very easily become materialistic. There are many odds to work against. There is a lot of superstition mixed in with the traditions of their culture. Last month we were talking about ouija boards. They know enough not to mess with them, but some will try, anyway.

All that is in the impoverished heart of Latin America comes here. They bring it with them. And they can only operate here on what they learned there. They cope. Good and evil—they need to choose.

It's very complicated, but that's where we are. Sometimes we feel we are stuck on a sand bar, not even sure how to get off. Then a wave of God's love hits us and we discover again that nothing is impossible with Him. For example: Gloria—one of *our* Christian kids graduated from high school, and was accepted at Reedley Junior College. There she met a young Christian international student from Guatemala. They are married now.

We are still learning.

NP: Thank you, Judy, for your honesty. I commend you for your faithful service. My prayer would be that every church would catch the vision of your ministry. And apply that vision to the needs of their community.

MISSIONARIES, OF ONE SORT

A number of years ago I was doing a seminar in a church. It was a seminar challenging the people to look beyond the *romanticism* of missions—and encouraging them to a personal involvement in cross-cultural ministry.[1]

Early in the afternoon session, the pastor was called out. At the time this didn't seem too unusual. Pastors are busy people.

When he returned later, though, he was obviously disturbed by something. They had a ministry among field workers. Several of the people in the housing complex where they met had been caught in some drug activity. INS had come and bused a bunch of them back to Mexico. Several of *their* families were caught up in that raid, though they had done nothing wrong. (Or did they? They were in the country illegally. But they were needed to work in the fields. It was harvest time.)

After he told his story of disappointment of losing these families—things had been going so well with a number of them, the thought came to me: "Pastor, you just had me doing a seminar encouraging your church to seriously get involved in the cross-cultural ministry of going into other countries. Though it didn't happen as you had expected it, you have just sent out your first missionaries!" That seemed to brighten his attitude a bit.

UNDERSTANDING THE ISSUES

The U.S. Immigration and Naturalization Service (INS) estimates up to eleven million persons attempt entering the United States illegally each year. Other estimates range from seven to twenty million people. About half are caught and returned to their country. Or, they are dropped off at the Mexican border, making their plight even worse. Many more enter and return to their home country on a regular basis. Of the 500,000-600,000 who become permanent illegal residents each year, up to 40% are those who have "overstayed" their legal visas!

Visa overstays are harder to track and much harder politically to deal with. Until recently, there was a backlog of 1.6 million people who had overstayed their visas. A new system of automation checks has reduced that number to 839,000. Of those, we are told that *only* about 2000 are determined as potential national security risks! Only!

(An interesting April 2013 side note: Saudi Arabia recently released a report of their issue with illegal aliens. They estimate the number to be in excess of five million people, in a total population of 29 million (17%). *Visa overstays* from the Haj and Umrah pilgrimages are the main reason for these large numbers. Illegal residents pose a large risk to the security of the Saudi Kingdom, as they are responsible for 60% of all reported crimes, including narcotics, liquor, robbery, murder, and the distribution of pornographic films. Additionally, they play a role in environmental pollution, the report from the Foreign Committee of the Shoura Council disclosed.

And a May 2013 follow-up: Far-reaching concessions have been made to absorb hundreds of thousands of "overstayers" who arrived in Saudi Arabia before July 3, 2008. Workers who entered the country illegally, however, will not benefit from these concessions. The illegal expatriate who does not leave the country will be jailed and fined. Employers who transport or shelter them will be punished with a two-year jail sentence and a fine of SR 100,000/$26,660.80).

Mexicans make up nearly 57% of the illegal population in the USA; 24% are from other Latin American countries. Nine percent are from Asia. This percentage is increasing at a faster rate than Latin America. Six percent are from Europe, 4% from other areas. Middle Easterners are one of the fastest growing immigrant groups in America. While the size of overall immigrant population has tripled, the number of immigrants from the Middle East has grown more than seven-fold.

Even with these statistics, it is commonly thought that this is a Mexico-southern United States "problem" with its 2000-mile border as the means of entrance for most. However, during one period of close checking,

75 nationalities were identified in the El Paso, Texas region. Nor are they staying in the southern regions of our country. "Oh, no," said a pastor friend in Juneau, Alaska, "we have several Latinos in our church. It is not easy to deal with them—even to first determine if they are illegal, then to sort out their story of political persecution or economic deprivation. They are living among us—all over the USA."

Despite the generous words inscribed on the pedestal of the Statue of Liberty, "Give me your tired, your poor, your huddled masses yearning to breathe free," the soul of America vacillates between welcoming them and resenting them. We turn a blind eye when we need more "cheap" labor but we also turn their boats back to Haiti when we don't want such "undesirables." We are caught in a cultural double mindedness. We want to open and close our borders at the same time.

Until 1970, legal immigration totals were 270,000 per year. This number could be absorbed into our culture and work force. Sensing the DINK phenomenon (double income, no kids), resulting in a dangerously low birth rate—close to the extinction of a culture (less than 2.1 per family), the number of *legal* immigrants was increased. By 1990, the number was over one million.

The Immigration Reform and Control Act of 1986 (modified in 1990) legalized 3.1 million foreigners (70% Mexican) who were able to meet certain criteria. By strict control on American industry, it was supposed to keep out any newcomers. The flood of illegal immigrants who followed such an openhearted amnesty program drowned out the cry of the law's opponents. It became nothing more than a gold-embossed invitation to those immigrants' relatives and friends. *Everyone* is a friend of one who has made it to El Norte!

The border between the United States and Mexico stretches 1,969 miles, crossing deserts, rivers, towns, and cities from the Pacific Ocean to the Gulf of Mexico. Every year, an estimated 350 million people legally cross the border, with another 500,000 entering into the United States illegally. No single barrier stretches across the entire border; instead, it is lined with a patchwork of steel and concrete fences, infrared cameras, sensors, drones, and nearly 20,000 U.S. Border Patrol agents. As immigrants from Mexico and other Central and South American countries continue to try to find their way into the U.S., Congress is again trying to frame a new immigration bill. The bill proposes solutions to current border enforcement problems and paths to citizenship for the estimated 11 million existing illegal immigrants in the U.S.

In a word, the borders are out of control. Every statistic is seeing a 15-20% increase each year. More money, more agents, 20-foot high steel and cement barricades and brilliant stadium lights along the border, assistance by the National Guard, vigilante posses— none of this is stemming the flood of humanity crossing over. They are coming from the south and east and west and north in a quest for the "good life." It is an empty, elusive dream. It is that "apple" that has been held out by the enemy from the beginning of time.

"To be truthful," Juan Luis said, "I have no idea where this train goes, other than that it takes us to El Norte!" He and his friend quickly slipped into the San Diego rail yard, furtively, under the protective cover of a moonless night. Jumping fences, evading guards and dodging 200-ton locomotives, they made a perilous dash for the most elusive of prizes—a free ride to the north.

Elsewhere along the porous 2000-mile border, undocumented migrants play a cat-and-mouse game with border agents. The dangers are real. By the time they get to the U.S., 65% of them have been robbed, beaten, extorted or raped by bandits or Mexican police.

Increasing brutality by the U.S. Border Patrol is further news fodder of pros and cons of this issue.

Yet, motivation is high; everyone who really wants to cross, ultimately does, or dies in the process. Employers are not checking documentation nor are they being fined for non-compliance. If fined, it is so low that it is still economically practical to employ illegals.

In cities around the country, there are thousands of known day-labor corners where workers congregate in the hope of gaining a day's work of pruning trees, hauling cement or mowing lawns.

Estimates are that as many as 7000 sweatshops operate in New York City and Los Angeles alone. Subpar working conditions in garment factories around the world have long been the subject of Stateside media attention, but conditions in American factories largely slip under the radar. Reports of working conditions and evidence of child labor offer eerie echoes of a previous time and generation. The truth is that sweatshops in America have been on the rise for the past several decades, highlighted by the $50 million lawsuit against Alexander Wang, which was silently settled and dismissed in 2012.[2]

In 1994, the North American Free Trade Agreement (NAFTA) was held as a hopeful "finger in the dike" against illegal immigration. By bolstering the Mexican economy, the pressures south of the border to migrate north would lessen. "It was only a familiar tune with reworked lyrics," many were warning. And today, thousands and hundreds of thousands of jobs have been exported south and north and west to China and other Asian countries to enjoy cheaper labor, no social security, no health insurance. Though NAFTA might be lauded for its free trade between Canada, the United States and Mexico, it did not stem the flow of illegal aliens!

More recently, not being able to get Congress to pass the Dream Act of 2012, the president extended and modified a *policy of prosecutorial discretion* that allowed about 800,000 young people who were brought to the U.S. illegally as children, to stay—with certain stipulations.

Still they come. A North San Diego County police study showed that 34% of their officers' time goes to illegals. Most contacts, however, involve minor or lesser offences. Yet, 94% of those who participated in the study said illegal aliens (undocumented residents) contribute to rising crime.

In Los Angeles, twenty years has shown an increase from 12% to 66% of felonies are committed by illegals. Ninety-five percent of all outstanding warrants for homicide are for illegal aliens. Two thirds of fugitive felony warrants are for illegals. Sixty percent of the 20,000 member 18th Street Gang of Southern California are illegals.

And not unlike Enrique and Rosa in the movie, "El Norte," they still come. Illegals make up about 6% of America's work force. Most do work nobody else will do, working for wages no one else will accept. More women are crossing alone or with just their children. Their own fears of being caught further erode the dream. They take different routes to work each day. When they are robbed or cheated by their employers, they can't go to the police for justice. No church, no recreation; just work. Huddled in canyons and under cement freeway bridges, they think the words of Moreno Rodriquez, "You feel like a piece of litter."

"Life is no better here," Jose Antonio concluded on his one-hundredth time to be caught and deported to Mexico. Like so many Oaxacans, Jose came to this country looking for work and a living wage, both of which he said he could not find in Mexico.

This time he says he is not coming back. He has had enough of infrequent jobs. Enough of dodging the

Border Patrol. Enough of masked robbers who invade the camps, stealing what little Jose and the other men have. Enough!

But he will probably be back. For all of his complaint, in 2012, $37 billion was wired to Mexico by individuals; $306 billion to other Latin American countries! This is a not insignificant drain on the American economy. Additionally, it is calculated that illegals cost American taxpayers $100 billion in services for which they contribute nothing in taxes. The nightmarish dream continues.[3]

ILLEGAL IMMIGRANT FROM BANGLADESH

It is Tuesday morning at Palomar College in San Marcos, September 1991. Students are settling into their classes. Campaign posters are up for the student elections. Loud rock music fills the student cafeteria. The Yogurt Shoppe is doing great business at 8 a.m.

In a corner of the cafeteria, Abu Ala Badruddoza, 26, illegal immigrant and self-described political refugee, is manning a card table. He has posters, a petition and a cause: himself!

He's fighting INS to avoid deportation to his native Bangladesh. He's seeking political asylum and says the ruling party will torture or kill him if he returns.

"I am not on welfare. I'm not doing a crime," he says. "All I want is to live in a democratic country."

Badruddoza says he is targeted as a political dissident by the military thugs who took over the Bangladesh government in the early 1980's.

He says he was arrested and tortured, and then began a journey that took him to several countries before he arrived in Mexico in 1988. From there it was a short sneak across the border.

He worked his way to Palomar, where he took courses for two semesters. He applied for political asylum.

The State Department says Badruddoza has not proven that he has an "actual and well-founded fear" of persecution. Neither he nor his lawyers have produced anything except his own word.

The significance of the 1991 story is this: Abu Ala Badruddoza, in 2012, is *still* fighting the system. Today it is with the IRS, who dismissed his appeal on the basis of a "lack of jurisdiction."[4]

ILLEGALS IN THE CLASSROOM

While doing research for this chapter, we entertained in our home a public school teacher friend of ours. I quoted some data I had read about illegals avoiding all public sector contact, including schools. The sounds of protest, and then finally, "Not true—not true!" led to this interview. Well, not so much an interview as a release valve blown! Bill teaches in a high school.

Bill: What are you talking about? The schools are filled with illegals, yet the principals cannot ask the parents for green cards. In fact, the parents are not even sought out. The kids just come and register themselves. They give the address of a cousin or aunt, or just an address. As long as that address is in my district, they're in!

NP: If they are obviously illegals, why can't they just not allow them in school?

Bill: The children are considered innocent of the problem; therefore, we are not to get them involved, so nothing is said. Once I did go to my principal. I was reprimanded for raising the subject. English-speaking kids in San Diego County are now in the minority. There are major changes taking place in the types of illegals showing up for class.

NP: What are those changes?

Bill: These are children of strictly economic immigrants—there is no religious or political motivation. They are younger, mentally. They have had little or no schooling. They don't know how to hold a pencil much less how to write their own name. Many don't even speak Spanish—only their Indian dialect, and that on a very young child's level, although they are in their teens. These are young adults without even kindergarten academic skills!

NP: What do you teach them?

Bill: Though I teach high school Spanish, I have to begin with these students at pre-kindergarten skills. I don't teach writing, but I have to use first grade, lined paper to help them form their letters between the lines. I don't teach math, but if they are going to understand just the dollar/peso exchange, I have to teach numbers. I don't teach history, but if they are going to understand their place in their new society, I have to teach them something about our past and theirs. Unless all the skills of full integration into mainstream society—even in its great diversity—can be taught to them within a year or a maximum of two, you get a whole sub-culture that develops living skills outside of acceptable parameters.

NP: Enlarge on that, please.

Bill: I mean, because they don't know how to fit in, they become bitter...hard...hate-filled. And they will fight at the sight of anyone who represents mainstream society. Our cities are laced with barrios of neglected kids trying to cope in a society they do not understand, a culture they did not choose, and a country in which their parents are trying to "get ahead." Each week, each month, each year more are appearing in our classrooms.

NP: How do you deal with such diversity in the classroom?

Bill: Certain objectives have been set for the class, it is true. It is difficult to meet those and yet spend time with the illegals. I will tutor before school and at lunch. But they just can't keep up with the English-speaking students because of their radical home life.

For example, they can't do their homework because they're taking care of younger brothers and sisters or helping their parents in their work; or there is no electricity where they live. I end up teaching two classes. Then the English-speaking students and their parents are furious because of allowances being made for the illegals. The school administration continues to ignore the problem.

NP: You remember that I used to teach in public schools, but I don't know if I could handle this.

Bill: Thanks for letting me say all of that, but there is another side. *(Note now how the true heart of a teacher is expressed.)* By the time I teach them how to write and spell and all.... As a teacher you receive more gratitude from them. They are vulnerable being out of their own environment and not being accepted by their English-speaking peers, so they appreciate even the littlest thing you do for them. They are so needy. Some have come across the border alone. Fourteen and fifteen-year olds sent by their families. They have put all of their hopes in this one getting across, learning English and getting a good job back home; or getting married and legally bringing the rest of the family across; or getting a good job here and sending money back home. How they miss their families; how lonely they are. In this continual state of mind, their chances of "making it" are not very good. Yes, they are living among us, even in our schools.

Bill concluded with, "I don't know a teacher who would not appreciate volunteers helping us in the classroom. I would!"

ILLEGALS IN *MY* HOME

Jorge is an amazing 7 year-old soccer player. Walnut colored skin, jet-black hair and a mile-wide smile with moves like Argentine footballer Leo Messi. He is also very protective of his younger brother Ramon and 2 year-old sister, Mia. Their father abandoned this Southern California family. Mom made a phone call to the Safe Families For Children hotline when she became homeless. They found a Christian family in Riverside County able to host all three children.

Jonathan tells his story:

> Jorge loved the nighttime Bible stories and began making plans to tell his new classmates about Jesus. His English is excellent and he translates the stories for his brother and sister into Spanish. A small problem appeared, however, when we learned that his mother did not have her green card and was not here legally. Different thoughts began creeping through our heads. Are we helping Maria remain here illegally by caring for her children? Is that the right thing to do? Are her children any different from other children in crisis?
>
> Our motivation and obedience were now under the scrutiny of the magnifying glass of immigration. When we became a host family with Safe Families For Children, nobody asked us if we were willing to host "illegal immigrant

children." Actually, the thought never entered our mind. Everyone needs the Gospel no matter where they live, what country they come from, or their legal status. We just wanted to serve the Lord by opening our home and hearts to children in need. It just seems like the right thing for a Christian family to do.

It really doesn't matter whether one is for or against illegal immigration. The real test is whether we allow society around us to shape our hearts with politics and/or prejudice. 'Maria's green card or lack thereof, is not the reason we are helping her children,' was our conclusion.

Does Maria face a very difficult situation? Absolutely she does. Can we help keep her family together during this crisis? Yes. Will they eventually move back to Mexico? Perhaps. What we do know is that Jorge has met Jesus and he plans on his classmates meeting Him as well. No matter how things work out for his mother, we are blessed to be a small part of their lives.[5]

ILLEGALS ON THE STREET CORNERS, BROTHELS AND SWEAT SHOPS

Slavery in the United States officially ended on January 1, 1863, freeing 1,775,515 slaves. However, globally, there are more people in the bondage of slavery today than in that year of President Lincoln's statement: *"That on the first day of January, in the year of our Lord one thousand eight hundred and sixty-three, all persons held as slaves...shall be then, thenceforward, and forever free...."*

An estimated 27 million men, women, and children are living in bondage somewhere in the world. In a recent year, slave traders made more profit than Google, Nike, and Starbucks combined. It's an estimated $35 billion industry, second only to drug trafficking.

- There are over one million new people trafficked annually.
- 80% are women, 50% of those are children.
- An estimated 100,000 minors are in the commercial sex trade in the United States.
- Every minute two children become victims of human trafficking.
- The average life span of a child caught in the sex slave trade is two years.
- They are either beaten to death, contract HIV/AIDS, contract bacterial meningitis, or overdose on drugs forced on them.[6]
- The average age of a child sexually exploited is 11. The average age of entry for a girl into prostitution is 13; for a boy, 12.[7]
- Southeast Asia is one of the world's largest exporters of sex slaves to brothels in Japan, China, Australia, Europe, and the *United States (emphasis added)*. Human traffickers are most successful in finding young girls among destitute rural villages. A child can be bought from its parents for as little as $25.
- An estimated 14,500 to 17,500 foreign nationals are trafficked into the United States each year. Victims pay to be illegally transported into the United States only to find themselves in bondage to traffickers. They are forced into prostitution, involuntary labor or other forms of servitude to repay debts—the cost of their illegal entry in the United States or some other real or contrived sum. With excessive interest charges, often the debt can never be paid in full. In certain cases, the victims are mere children brought in with false documentation as children of the smugglers. They find themselves surrounded by an unfamiliar culture and language without

identification documents, fearing for their lives and the lives of their families.[8]

A simple Google search would bring you more statistics about sex slaves that you would care to read. These, too, are illegal aliens living among us. The challenge I put before you is what are you going to do about it? An initial action is to keep your eyes open for the following common trafficking indicators:

- Victim does not have ID or travel documents.
- Victim has been coached in how to talk to law enforcement and immigration officials.
- Victim is in a forced labor situation or sex trade.
- Victim's salary is garnished to pay off smuggling fees.
- Victim is denied freedom of movement.
- Victim or family is threatened with harm if escape is attempted.
- Victim is threatened with deportation or arrest.
- Victim has been harmed or denied food, water, sleep or medical care.
- Victim is denied contact with friends or family.
- Victim is not allowed to socialize or attend religious services.[9]

Once a slave is rescued... I had to pause after writing that. It is inconceivable to me that in this post-everything society, that by FBI estimates, there are as many as 100,000 human trafficking victims in the U.S. who are currently enslaved! Once you have been able to rescue one who has suffered enslavement, there are certainly physical needs to be met. But beyond meeting physical needs lies a major area of ministry: Addressing the spiritual injuries and trauma they have endured. In addition to helping them materially, legally, or in some other practical way, they need to experience the healing of the Great Physician. They are people for whom Christ died. They are people who need to know the love of Jesus Christ. They need your incarnational *agape* love. One of the open doors to an effective ministry relationship is the simple question, "May I pray for you?"

There are Christian or civic organizations to which you could lend your support. Again, the Internet is a source for choosing an organization. Care must be given in selecting one. Make sure they are giving aid in the Name of Jesus. Better still, this is a ministry for *you* and your church.

These next five suggestions of what you can do about slavery are a summary of a blog by Ben Reaoch:

First, he reminds us that the trafficker of slaves is also himself enslaved to lust for power and money. All involved in this industry, including the one who buys the slave, were created to worship God. Each soul is valuable to Him.

- Pray! Pray for the estimated 27 million slaves in our world today who are in bondage within affluent countries like America to Third-world countries like Haiti. (At this writing, the conviction and trial of a man in America who held three girls as slaves for over ten years might still be on our minds. But in two months, what will be the new statistic?)
- Raise awareness. People need to know that this is happening, so it can be observed and reported and prosecuted. *The Slave Next Door* by Kevin Bales[10] will open anyone's eyes to the enormity and vileness of this industry.
- Don't look at porn. Pornography is the gateway drug to deeper involvement. Users heighten the demand, which then motivates the producers to exploit even more people to provide the pictures.
- Use your gifts. In every arena of community service, you can use your position to make an impact:

politician, lawyer, police officer, businessperson, mentor or neighbor. The ultimate path to recovery is the Gospel of Jesus Christ.

• Men, take a stand. Slavery today mainly harms women and girls. And it's mainly men who are the abusers. There need to be Christian men who will speak out against abuse, exploitation, pornography and prostitution.[11]

THE LEGAL FACTOR

Rhetoric is cheap. It flows from the pens and mouths of the jaundiced. We seem to have activists for every cause. "Save the whales," some shout. In syncopated harmony others blend their voices with "Save the spotted owls—the snails—spiders! Trees! Plants have feelings, too!" What about the feelings of cockroaches?

While society drowns in the floods of verbal attacks, thousands—millions of precious souls are dying, lost without a Savior. Jesus knew how to avoid these "flesh and blood" battles. To the man who wanted Him to get involved in his issue of earthly inheritance, Jesus said, *"Who made Me a ruler and judge over you...."* (See Luke 12:13-14.)

Jesus knew His priorities. And He maintained a steadfast focus on them.

The legal factor of illegal aliens could become an all-consuming "flesh and blood" issue. I have read the arguments. I have considered the options. I have come to the conclusion that while politicians argue their agendas and activists plot their procedures, I will acknowledge these aliens as eternally significant people for whom Christ died, for whom the heart of God beats, *"Not willing that any perish, but that all come to repentance"* (II Peter 3:9). And for whom I should expend my energies to *"...open their eyes, turn them from darkness to light, from the power of satan to God, so that they may receive forgiveness of sins, and an inheritance among them, which are sanctified by faith that is in Me"* (Acts 26:18).

One church reasoned, "As long as the world exists with such a grossly disproportionate distribution of wealth, we will never stop the flood of people coming across our borders. "Give me your tired, your poor, your huddled masses yearning to breathe free" is still deep in the soul of America. The poor and downtrodden of the world will come. We can't stop them. We can't ignore them. Our only option is to minister to them.

How? "How do I get involved?" you may be asking in light of all these statistics. Here are two ideas:

In our area, the unregistered aliens live in cardboard shacks in canyons. One such group lives just over the hill from our church. They are periodically rounded up and returned to Mexico. It takes them about a day or two to make it back.

We now have individual headsets for simultaneous translation of our services. But before that, they would sit in the foyer of the church watching a TV monitor with an interpreter sitting with them. One evening, to the surprise of us all, when the pastor invited people to come forward for the pastors and elders to lay hands on and pray for all who wished, eight men came down the center aisle. Ushers went scrambling to find bi-lingual workers to accompany each to an elder or pastor!

Mario has become a real evangelist. He is bold. He is alive. He is compassionate. He is intense. He is illegal! We have sponsored him and have given him 30 hours of work a week. We are in the process of helping him get his proper documentation.

A couple in North County cut through the "legal factor" by saying,

> As Christians, we have a moral commitment. It's as simple as that. Our struggle is with the enormity of the need. It is easy to become overwhelmed—and do nothing! But at those times, we are encouraged by a statement of one who got the world's attention by her simple demonstration of God's love: "You do what you can with what you have, NOW!" Notable words of Mother Theresa.
>
> No, we are not going to solve the total problem. No, we are not going to work so hard and long that we burn out. But neither are we going to say the project is too big so that we end up doing nothing.
>
> What do we do? We prepare 200 sandwiches every Saturday and distribute them along the streets where the men and boys are waiting for work. When the sandwiches are gone, we go home. But God's Word says that long after those sandwiches are eaten, the Bread of Life that we gave them will be nourishing (or convicting) their souls. And that's what it's all about!

THE FEAR FACTOR

You have come with us this far on our journey to understand the diverse groups of internationals who live among us. You do not want to have just read *another* book about these people. You want to become intentional in some action with one group or another. At this point, I would like to challenge you to come to grips with what may be called—the fear factor. We certainly are aware of internationals living among us. We cannot walk into a congested mall or park or wait at a busy street corner without hearing the sounds of many languages and seeing the skin color of many nations. Why do we avoid relating with them? Why do we seek our own kind? Why do we hide behind any one of the following statements, letting it induce fear in us? Let's play Twenty Questions! On a scale of 1 to 5 (with 5 being the most severe fear factor), please evaluate yourself. This is not a national survey—I have only just taken the challenge myself. I would say that a total score of 60 or more should send us to our closet of prayer, asking God for boldness to share the Good News!

WHY HAVE I NOT TAKEN UP THE BANNER FOR INTERNATIONALS WHO LIVE AMONG US?
1) I fear to even become aware of them: ____
2) I fear that if I get involved, it will consume my time: ____
3) My leaders fear, thus don't talk about them or encourage me to relate with them: ____
4) I fear that I won't know what to do: ____
5) I fear offending their culture: ____
6) I fear that I don't know how to talk with them: ____
7) I fear that I don't understand them: ____
8) I am just simply afraid of them: ____
9) I fear relating takes too much effort: ____
10) I fear rejection: ____
11) It is a special ministry for others, not me: ____
12) They have their own religion and I have mine: ____
13) They don't like us: ____
14) They are so different from us: ____
15) They have come to take over; we need to protect ourselves: ____
16) They don't respect us or our way of life: ____
17) We are to be separate and come out from them: ____
18) I am called to expose false religions and heresies, not encourage them: ____

19) I fear for my family and need to protect them from their influences: ____

20) I am busy doing God's other work: ____

Sixty, or more? Let's find that closet of prayer.

We have just grappled with one of the most difficult to deal with groups of internationals who live among us. There are no easy answers. Yet, the high road is the moral road. They are here. Let the politicians deal with the legal issues. While they are here among us, let's introduce them to Jesus and disciple them well, so that, when they are "caught" or when they voluntarily return to their own country with a vision to share Christ, they will be able to stand strong in their conviction.[12]

But there are other internationals who live among us. In the next chapter, we want to explore ministry among a group of internationals who are usually with us for a very brief period of time. And who might be more difficult to identify.

"Don't open it up unless you're willing to follow it up."
That little bit of down-to-earth philosophy easily could
have come from Ben Franklin's Almanac. But it didn't.
It is wisdom that God had worked deep into the heart
of Mick Ewing, pastor of Calvary Fellowship in Juneau,
Alaska, and God put him to the test to see how firmly it
was fixed there. It happened this way:

The whole city of Juneau, Alaska was alive with
anticipation of the arrival of 150 visitors from their sister
city, Vladivostok, USSR. The time was April of 1991,
five months before the Soviet coup d'état attempt. The
city fathers had decided to begin building a friendship
exchange. This was something new. It was exciting. But
there was risk, and thus caution.

The caution was exercised when Pastor Mick,
representative of the Juneau Evangelical Pastors
Fellowship asked if they could present each visitor with
a Bible as they disembarked from the plane. The answer
was, "No!" Not to be daunted by that "apparent" closed
door, he persisted. So they were given a book table in a
downtown building that would be used as the hub—a
rendezvous—for these visitors. A snack bar was also set
up in that building.

The Fellowship went into high gear to find and secure
any and all Christian literature written in Russian: Whole
Bibles, New Testaments, Children's Bibles, two excellent
books, *More than A Carpenter* and *Knowing God.* They
also secured a variety of tracts, music tapes (Ed: This

was before CDs.), and T-shirts with Christian messages. They were ready, they thought!

The visitors came. They looked at the snack bar. They looked at the book table. Visitor after visitor made his priority choice; they came to the book table to receive the *Living Food* of God's Word. Over 700 Bibles, books and numerous tracts later, they ran out. Desperate calls were made to purchase more Children's Bibles. That is what they kept asking for. "Please! Can't you give us more Bibles for our children?"

Mick reported, "Our American (Christian?) sense of right and wrong made us wonder whether all of these books would end up on the black market. Stories had been told of Bibles being sold and sold again, the price escalating each time. 'The visitors would have to deal with that,' we decided. Our prayer was that God would bless the people who received and read them."

Having put that in the Lord's hands, they relaxed and began relating with the people. The table was being manned all hours of the day and evening. They had never seen such spiritual hunger. Just the simple gesture of giving them a gift disarmed them. "Why are you doing this for us?" they kept asking. The Lord was opening the Russians' hearts.

One lady approached the table curiously. When she saw the Bibles, she quietly said, "I'm a Christian." Mick's response was raised hands and a spontaneous, "Praise the Lord!" Without thought, the lady also raised her hands and gave a burst of praise. Startled by what she had done, she quickly dropped her hands. She looked around cautiously, wondering—afraid of who might have seen her. "Political officers," she whispered in a language Pastor Mick didn't understand. He could only guess from her gesture over her shoulder. Political officers were assigned to each ship or plane—just to make sure everyone was being a "good" communist. Had one accompanied this group's tour?

Yes, one had: Vladimir. Of course he didn't introduce himself to Mick as one. No, rather, as a merchant marine. It was the other visitors calling him the outcast that let it be known that he was a hard-line communist—the political officer.

"I'm too old to change," was his first response to Mick's quest to introduce him to Jesus. "No one is too old!" "But I'm an atheist!" was his next retort. "I don't believe in atheism," Mick replied. And a relationship was forming.

Over the book table was a banner, "Jesus Is Risen From The Dead." Mick had taken a picture of Vladimir, which coincidentally framed him right in the arc of that banner. When he was shown the picture, he said, "You're trying to get Jesus into my head!" "No!" Mick responded. "We would like to see Him come into your heart." By the end of the week, Vladimir asked for prayer.

The visitors went home. The people of Calvary Fellowship wondered at the excitement of that week. They waited. A specially printed bookmark had been placed in each Bible and book given. Within weeks, letters began coming. "Where can we find more of these books—especially the Children's Bibles?" An ongoing communication with three pastors was developing. A lot of work and time to get letters translated? YES. To understand each other? YES. To be committed to what might develop? YES!

Vladimir sent Mick a package with a book, *The History of the Russian Orthodox Church.* An ongoing communication developed with him. In another letter, he said, "My home is open to you. Please stay with me when you visit." 'When you *visit*,' Mick pondered. 'What is going to come of this?'

But a relationship of much greater proportion and significance than just "sister cities" had been opened up. And now God's testing of "Are you willing to follow up what you opened up?" was upon the Fellowship. It was determined that the next step would be to go over there and meet with the pastors and others who were asking them to come.

Alex, a Vladivostok newspaper editor, had been on the original visit to Juneau. Now that he heard Mick and the others were in town, he searched them out. "You must come to my home for dinner."

"During our time in Vladivostok," Mick said, "he wrote two articles about what we were doing. They were both very positive. One was titled, 'Christians have come to share good news with our people.'"

Mick continued: "It only snowballed from there. We were aware of Campus Crusade and Intensive Care Ministry, of CBN and Bill Gothard accepting invitations from the now wide-open Commonwealth republics. We thought, being so close to Russia's back door, we would slip in that way. We even decided to call our efforts the Back Door Ministry. But before long, as other churches wanted to link arms with us, we realized it would be bigger than that. Effectual Door (See I Corinthians 16:9.) was considered as a name. Then others who were targeting Belorussia wanted to join us. Now it looked like God had opened a back door, front door, and even some side doors!

"Though we have certainly learned not to 'box' God into any plans, we were moving in the direction of two short-term trips in May and July, doing the Intensive Bible Study seminar in Vladivostok, and two other major cities in the area. By January of '93, our plans were to have a team of six strategically located. By summer of '93, an in-country training for others who would live and work closely with the pastors who take the Intensive Bible Study training was being considered.

Pastor Mick concluded, "It was only going to be a small gesture of Christian good will as part of our city welcoming international visitors from the Soviet Union. Only time will tell what all God has for us as we try to 'follow up on what we, by His grace, opened up.'" Posted: January 1992.

"God's timetable, not ours. God's agenda, not ours. God's glory, not ours!" These were Pastor Mick's first words to me at the beginning of a September 2012 phone call. By email I had asked him to bring me up to date with what God had opened up for him and his fellowship. What an amazing "follow up" that is *still* following up!

Mikhail Gorbachev's original goal of using glasnost (freedom of speech) and perestroika (restructuring) to reform the Soviet Union was not achieved. A failed coup by hard-line communists in August of 1991 eventually led to the dissolution of the Soviet Union. (Excuse the oversimplification of a complex period in the history of the USSR.)

The floodgates were open. Ministries of every stripe were rushing in. Leaders felt certain that an open door of opportunity would not remain for long.

Pastor Mick recalls, "We were overwhelmed with joy at how God had orchestrated that initial visit—how the Slavic Gospel Association had provided Bibles and Children's Bibles and tracts, how the Josh McDowell ministry had provided copies of his book, *More Than a Carpenter*, frantic phone calls to get more literature to hand out, how FedEx made special expedited shipments to fill the hands of precious souls with God's Word, the communist 'political officer' trusting in Christ...." Memorable thoughts kept pouring out as the pastor recalled those events of so many years ago. It had to have been a mind-boggling, ecstatic week of divine-ordained happenings.

Within weeks letters were coming, asking for more material—especially Children's Bibles. Come over and help us! It was as clear a Macedonian Call as Paul and his team had received that night in Troas.

The next opportunity for "follow up" came when the City of Juneau decided to return the friendship by chartering a plane to Vladivostok. Pastor Mick and six members of his congregation joined the city fathers and other residents of Juneau on that first trip. Realizing that this jumbo jet would have ample cargo space, permission was asked for and granted to take material. The Evangelical Pastors Fellowship got behind the project. Through two praise gatherings announcing this venture, $10,000 was raised to purchase fifty boxes of Bibles. More tracts, more books. "We were ready for...we didn't know what," Mick expressed.

He continued, "We went and our eyes were opened. We were blown away!" At the time, Vladivostok was a city of one million people. It was the USSR's Pacific naval port. Because of the intense military presence, it was a closed city. Travel in and out of the city was restricted, even for family members from other cities who wanted to visit their relatives. It was even more controlled for people from the United States. "But we were there! Ambassadors from the USA, but more than that, ambassadors of our Lord Jesus Christ!" Mick laughed with exuberance over the phone, even these many years later.

The Bibles and tracts that had been picked up in Juneau had evidently been sent out from Vladivostok or picked up by visiting relatives. They were receiving letters and invitations from Magadan, 80 kilometers to the south and from Khabarovsk, 150 kilometers to the north.

But one letter seemed to Mick to be of particular significance. In fact, in those few months a number of letters had gone back and forth with one man. Mick sensed in this man a strong desire to see "follow up." When Mick knew of the good-will sister-city trip, he again wrote to Nicholo: "We are not wanting to 'import' American Christianity. Try to find local church leaders who would want us to work with them. We would like to discover how we might help."

Of course, there was no phone directory listing of churches. Nor a city welcome pack with a list of churches at which you might want to fellowship. But through much person-to-person searching, he wrote that he had found six churches. Not six who were willing to meet, but just a total of six churches in a city of one million! And all six wanted to meet.

"We were very busy with sister-city activity," Mick remembers, "but in our free time we met with these church leaders. Our thought was to provide the materials and help these leaders 'reach their city' for Christ.

"How easily we take freedom for granted. Though a measure of freedom of speech (glasnost) was being written about, we found the people were bound in the fear that decades of mental and emotional imprisonment had created. Unfortunately, fear and, probably distrust of Americans, left us with only two of the churches wanting our help: The unregistered Baptist and the Pentecostal. They were excited and wanted to reach out to their city, but they had no idea about how to share their faith openly."

I interjected: "About this same time—shortly after 'the Wall' came down—at the request of local church leaders, my wife led an evangelistic team to several Eastern European countries: A music group, a creation teacher, a children's teacher, an evangelist and a photographer. They would set up in the town square and begin singing. They encouraged the local believers to join in. At one point, a local pastor standing next to my wife exclaimed, as if it was a brand new insight—a wild revelation, '*We* can do this!'"

Pastor Mick continued, "The drabness of a dismal city of broken power and water lines was reflected in the gray and dark clothing worn by the residents. We watched as, one by one, they towed rusting and listing warships out to deep water to sink them. But on a much deeper level, we saw the hopelessness of a system of government that had left the people bankrupt of anything positive.

"That week left an indelible mark on us," Mick spoke with determination. "We spent as much time as possible with the people of those two churches, helping them hand out Bibles. We left the rest of the material with Nicholo to share between the two churches."

At this point in the phone conversation, Pastor Mick was recalling these events with such excitement that his words just came tumbling out. "Wait a minute...slow down," I had to say.

"We had to do something more. There had to be a return trip. What we—no, what God had opened up, we knew that we had to follow up."

It was a "heady" time! A jubilant time! News of Co-Mission receiving open door invitations to teach thousands of public school teachers how to teach morals and ethics based on the Bible increased the excitement. They were doing the training in Magadan and Khabarovsk. Through Mick's contacts in those cities, he was able to arrange for them to teach the public school teachers in Vladivostok, as well. Yes, a great impact was being made in this vast country—from the Ural Mountains to the Pacific Ocean.

Others were joining in Mick's enthusiasm. International flights were not yet flying into Vladivostok. So they flew to Magadan and took the Trans-Siberian train to Vladivostok. Again, everywhere they went, they handed out Bibles. But the response often was, "What is a Bible?" They just didn't realize what they were holding in their hands. So, sometimes with a translator and sometimes by just pointing to the stories in the Bible and letting them read, they had to slowly walk them through the Truth of God's creation, His love for His creation, Jesus' birth and death and resurrection—the simplest of Bible stories. The people listened with eager ears and hearts to receive. This was all so new.

While participating in a Stateside conference of church leaders, being taught and encouraged to walk through this wide-open door of the USSR, God had a little talk with Mick. Over many years, as they raised their three children, he and his wife had been able to save $10,000. He had always wanted to invest in stocks. With this amount, he was now ready. But God said, "What's wrong with *My* investment portfolio?" Needless to say, that money went to purchase more Bibles and airline tickets for another trip.

During one of Mick's team trips, the Operation Mobilization ship, Doulos, made a port of call at Vladivostok. The Doulos became the second non-Soviet ship to ever enter this port, home of the Soviet Union's Pacific Fleet. The Doulos itself was a floating bookshop that sailed the world to spread knowledge, help, hope and salvation. But for this destination, Mick was able to coordinate the receiving of a whole ocean container of packaged libraries of Christian books. They were allowed to hold school assemblies, share the Good News, and present each school with this library of new books.

Pastor Mick was now ready for a larger team—a group of 20. Nicholo set it up. But, what? Where? Not in Vladivostok? A retreat center? Mick was thinking, "We are coming to minister, not to have a vacation!" But his initial disappointment gave way to ecstatic elation!

In the USSR, there are huge health resorts. People come to these massive hotels from all over the vast country for their one-week government-paid vacation. This one was by the Pacific Ocean. On their very first day, the team came out of their door, sat on the expansive steps and began playing their guitars and singing. And the people came! They carried the park benches and put them in front of the building. As the vacationers listened to the music—a few even joining in by clapping—other team members began passing out Bibles and copies of the Jesus Film. Now, not only was their follow up to the people of Vladivostok, as had been planned, but God's Word was going out to cities throughout the whole region. They were able to focus on seven cities. They found Christian leaders from those seven cities and met with them. They prayed with them. While working with these people, commitments were made to establish a Bible Study in each of their cities. Several were sure that they could get the Jesus Film on their local TV station.

In the years following, continuing to work with Nicholo, these seven cities and others, had churches established, and they, in turn, were adopting other cities in which fellowships could be established.

Has that simple Vladivostok-Juneau sister-city outreach been sufficiently "followed-up" yet? No! Not by God's plan. Now, in His Master Plan, it was time to send a team for a longer-term commitment to Vladivostok. Shortly after the team was settled into their homes and ministries, it was my privilege to join them for three weeks at that health resort for some intense cultural and interpersonal relationship training.

Coincidently, at that same time, another group was using that facility to gather high school students for a free three-week training in morals and ethics—based on the teachings of Sun Myung Moon! Yanko, the translator, was a Bulgarian. He was translating from English into Russian.

Though the dining hall was enormous with a thousand or more eating at the same time, word came to me at one lunchtime: "Yanko wanted to talk with me," I was told. Knowing whom he represented and, no doubt, what he wanted to talk about, I said, "Yes, I would be happy to, on one condition: We will only talk about 'What have you done with Jesus.'" We had three long walks and talks along the Pacific shore. He knew the King James Bible—extremely well! We discussed many things about Jesus.

However, at the end of our third walk, knowing it would be our last, he said, "I know you will be disappointed by what I am about to say, but I still believe Reverend Moon is my true heavenly father." At the end of this assignment, Yanko was headed for a mass wedding, to be married to a woman from South America whom he had never met!

I wonder where Yanko is today with his "heavenly father" dead.

Time passes. Missionaries fulfill their commitments. People are being established in the Word and reaching out to family and friends. But God's Plan of "follow-up" is still not yet complete! There was a new stirring in Mick's heart to relinquish his pastorate and take his wife and daughter to Vladivostok. His two sons were adults and decided to stay in America. Mick's plan was to establish a small Bible society for the distribution of Bibles and Christian books. But the new priority would be establishing solid Bible study, learning *how* to study the Bible, developing home Bible study groups and see them grow into church fellowships.

"*I* was going to orchestrate a bookshop, Chords of Love," Mick stated on that phone call with a clear emphasis on the word, "I"! "But God...He is so phenomenal!" Mick continued. "I had been shaking this same tree (his American church) for ten years waiting for *one* apple to fall. I had prayed for years, in travail and languishing—for fruit. And now, hundreds of apples were sitting on the ground, waiting for us to gather them up and put them in bushels of home Bible study groups."

His memory stirred, Mick went on: "I remember one day—we went to this place often—as we were standing in the front of a huge statue of Lenin with a case of Bibles, we would say to those passing by, 'I want to give you a Bible and tell you about the God of the Bible.' Sometimes when the word spread that there were Bibles at the feet of Lenin, and all the Bibles were gone, we would have to make a quick exit to avoid being mobbed."

Pastor Mick went to start a small Bible society shop, but God said, "I will establish an empire—I will build My Church!"

With such a positive story, you may wonder, "Could this all happen without some problems?" Unfortunately, all did *not* go well. I was called to conduct that three-week training because the team had not had pre-field training and were experiencing some interpersonal relationship problems, which was not a good witness. It was vital for them to learn these principles of relationships, since Jesus did say, "They will know that you are *My* disciples by your *love for one another*" (John 13:35).

Also, Nicholo, who was so instrumental in the progress for years, was tempted to take control. And he tried. And not unlike others who have followed the desire for power, the ministry went "sideways" for a while. "It's hard to define," Mick lamented. "But his vision was so small; *he* wanted to be in control. When a leader is doing so well, it is difficult to leave the direction in God's hands. We had to disassociate with him. Unfortunately, there were some church splits. Some churches decided they did not want to reach out; others did. It's just hard to define...." Mick was obviously struggling to put into words the sorrow of broken fellowship.

But, as we came to the end of our phone call, Mick's words again began to tumble out as he reminisced on this magnificent venture of faith. "God's picture is so much bigger than ours. The churches are still going out to villages—some of them are way up north. And those in leadership are doing outreaches to other villages from those outposts."

I asked what happened to Vladimir, that "political officer" on their first visit to Juneau. "Oh, Vladimir! He is one of the key elders. Years ago, this burly 'merchant marine' came to me to be baptized. 'Now!' he declared, in a voice not to be argued with! It was winter. Trying to make my voice sound as firm as his, I said, 'We are *not* going out to the ocean!' We filled the bathtub with water. We finally got him totally submersed. Not all at once," Mick laughed. "When his head went down, his knees came up!"

They knew Mick had pastored a church named Calvary Fellowship. They wanted to please him by naming their churches after his. He emphatically said, "There was no way we were going to call the churches there, 'Fellowship of the Skull'! They still write to me: 'Won't you come on back and help us.' No, I state emphatically, it is fully Russian now!"

Mick ended with this story: "You know, one of my fondest memories happened in a village some distance from Vladivostok. We had brought a case of Bibles for them to share with friends and family. In exchange... here his voice broke in tenderness...they gave me a hand-copied Bible and hymnbook, written down from memory. Oh, not the entire Bible, but all they could collectively remember during those dark days of oppression."

Then, in a reflective voice, Mick said, *"And to think all of this started by extending a hand of friendship to a group of international visitors."*

HOSPITALITY: A MEANS TO WIN THE LOST

One may ask, "Is hospitality really effective evangelism?" Is it possible that hospitality is a distraction from better, more effective, approaches? Or worse, another excuse to not getting on with the "real" work? Does it seem like Christians often will do almost anything but share the Gospel? Would they rather study evangelism than do it? Would they rather write about it than do it? Would they even rather pray about it than do it? Is hospitality another example of a Christian's aversion to obeying God's command to "go preach?"

"Not at all," says Gregg Harris. "There is mounting evidence that hospitality is a major means by which people come to Christ. Researchers have found 70-90 percent of all Christians became followers of Christ through contact with friends and relatives."[1] The explosion of the Chinese Church has been, not through crusades or televangelists but rather through one family member to another family member, house to house sharing of the liberation from darkness into the Kingdom of Light.

It was my privilege to pass through three security checkpoints before entering the twenty-first floor penthouse home of Moses. His twelve other guests arrived one by one. By the time I was introduced to the fourth or fifth guest, I stopped trying to calculate the net worth of these executives. It was mind-boggling! They were presidents of conglomerates... officers of international banks... industry magnates. I sat down. One gentleman sat down next to me. When he turned to me, his very first words were, "I'm a new baby! I am the newest baby here. I just trusted in Jesus two weeks ago." He told me that many members of his family were already Christians. I asked him, "Why did you wait so long?" He smiled, hesitated, he himself wondering why and said, "I don't know!" We laughed, and the dinner began. These businessmen were friends of Moses. His gift of hospitality brought six Christians and six "soon-to-be" Christians into his home!

Hospitality may mean giving a glass of water to a repairman, inviting a neighbor for a meal or hosting international guests for a few days. Hospitality opportunities are everywhere. Make yourself available to be God's warmth of friendship to the "strangers who live among us."

The Bible and ancient Jewish tradition show a strong basis for modern-day hospitality that can draw people to Jesus. The Torah commanded the Hebrews to be hospitable to all strangers. *"When a stranger resides with you in the land, you will do him no wrong. The stranger who resides with you will be as the native among you, and you will love him as yourself; for you were once aliens (strangers) in the land of Egypt; I am the Lord your God"* (Leviticus 19:33-34).

The Old Testament Jew was to receive, feed, lodge and protect any traveler who stopped at his door. Listen to Moses talking about Abraham: *"So he (Abraham) lifted up his eyes and looked, and behold, three men were standing by him; and when he saw them, he ran from the tent door to meet them, and bowed himself to the ground, and said, 'My Lord, if I have found favor in Your sight, do not pass by Your servant. Please let a little water be brought, and wash your feet, and rest yourselves under the tree. And I will bring a morsel of bread, that you may refresh your hearts. After that you may pass by, inasmuch as you have come to your servant.' They said, 'Do as you have said'"* (Genesis 18:2-5). And he prepared not just a "morsel" of bread, but a whole dinner!

By the times of Jesus, such hospitality had become a well-established custom. If a traveler should stop beside the door, the homeowner was to offer food and lodging without the stranger even asking. Cleopas and his wife, Mary, met a "Stranger" on the road as they were returning to their home in the village of Emmaus. It was toward evening, so they insisted on bringing this Stranger to their home for an evening meal and a night's lodging (Luke 24:13-35).[2]

Mary, Martha and Lazarus repeatedly opened their home to Jesus and His disciples. Paul, welcoming Cornelius' messengers into Simon's home is further example of this practice (Act 10). Probably the greatest infraction of this custom is told in Jesus' story of the "rich man and Lazarus." The rich man refused even the most basic considerations of hospitality (Luke 16:19-25).

Brazilians hang a wall carving in the entrance hall of their homes. It shows a front doorframe to a house with the door partly open. It is a clear message of hospitality. We have one hanging in our entrance hallway.

One evening we were seated for dinner. Our guests were Andy and his father, both from China, and the pastor of a local Chinese church. Our friend in Beijing had arranged this. Andy was to play in a golf tournament here. Our friend said he could arrange housing for them if they promised to go to church with us. Just as we were ready to pray, the doorbell rang. He was not a stranger to my wife and myself, but a most unusual sight to all of us. He had had a friend drop him off at the Mexican border. He planned to walk home—forty-five miles to the north. He had taken four days and three nights to get to our house. He had slept under bridges and on park benches. His food had been scavenged from restaurant throw-aways. To make things appear worse, his hair was in the wildest dreadlocks style. He was dirty. He smelled. He was tired. He was lonely. "Could I please take a shower and sleep tonight on your living room floor?"

Of course, our guests, strangers among us, were waiting for the prayer before eating. They sat dumbfounded! We could only guess what was going on in their minds as they watched our response to his request. "Ronny, come on in. You must be hungry. We're just about to eat. Join us." He did take a shower first which made him a bit more presentable to our guests. Only eternity will tell if that act of kindness had anything to do with the father trusting in Christ as Savior after he returned to China. He did insist on me being his guest next time I am in Beijing.

A friend from the Middle East wrote, "Two college-aged Muslims walked into Pastor Aahil's church last Sunday. They enjoyed the service and stayed after to have tea and to talk with Pastor Aahil. He asked how they had come to attend his church that day. They said they were on vacation recently on the west coast of America and had had conversations with some Christians. The American Christians were so warm and friendly that it had made a strong impression on these two young men. When they returned to their university in Beirut, they searched for a Christian church online and found Pastor Aahil and the Protestant Church. We pray for these young men to continue their path to Jesus."

Did those American Christians realize the impact of their behavior? Probably not, yet God orchestrated that brief contact with international visitors for His glory.

Walter Best, president of Best Lock Corporation (now BEST Access Systems) in the mid- to late Twentieth Century, operated his company as a committed Christian. This included leading his staff in daily prayer and Bible devotions. It also extended to showing great hospitality to those visiting his company. If one were to visit Best Lock for a tour, Mr. Best would ask during the course of conversation, "Do you pray? Do you need prayer? Do you know Jesus?" It didn't matter if the visitor was a child from a local school or from a corporation or a prospective client from Saudi Arabia, Mr. Best treated each of his guests to his overt Christian hospitality.

He told one startled young man visiting the plant that one convert to Christ was better than the sale of 100,000 locksets.[3]

Let even another story solidify in your mind the importance of friendship as the "door" to evangelism:

A couple met a Muslim man who owned a small import store in the States. They would drop by his shop occasionally to have a neighborly conversation with him. They became friends and introduced him to many of their friends. They invited him over for dinner, asking him to share about his country and his culture. He enjoyed himself so much that he would often visit, bringing many of his Muslim friends along so they too could get to know some Americans. The relationships developed easily because of the genuine interest and love shown to these people from other countries.

After a few months, this man came over one night, broken and in tears. He'd been observing the freedoms his friends have in America— especially the religious freedom they enjoy. He was in despair because his family had "arranged a marriage" for him—to someone whom he could not love. His life was falling apart and in that crisis he turned to the only friends he knew would help him. That door of friendship led him to the door of salvation, for he gave his heart to the Lord.[4]

Using your own hospitality for evangelism will not replace the globe-spanning efforts to reach the unsaved for Christ. Translating the Bible into the Pago Pago language is important for those people to read in their own language the Truth about the Kingdom of Light. But the first step into world evangelism for *you* is at the doorstep of your home.

Is your home your "castle;" closed and private—a haven from the outside world? If so, it might be good for you to ask the Lord to change your heart. To open your heart and your door to the stranger who comes to live among us, even for such a brief time as a visit.

Seriously consider what the writer of Hebrews says, *"Do not forget to entertain strangers, for by so doing some have unwittingly entertained angels"* (Hebrews 13:2).

ONE LADY'S ANSWER

She pondered: How do I help international visitors feel more at home in my community? What are the opportunities that fit my personality and ability? What can I do to *"Love them as myself"?* What can I do for the international tourist who is "alien" in our country for just a brief visit?

"As I mulled over this issue and the clear Scriptural injunction to befriend and love them—and as I thought of my own interest in the culture and attractions in my hometown—an idea began to germinate: Provide a tourist touring service.

"I began researching. What are the unique characteristics of my area? What brings (or could bring) visitors here? Do we have spots of historical, political or cultural interest? Do we have a rare species of flora or fauna? Are there unique geologic formations? Do we have distinctive cultural mores, such as folk dances, houses or dress styles? Do we have an industry (cheese making, etc) that would be interesting to tour? Do we have clear skies without ozone holes? A place to relax and enjoy life?

"I was able to say, *yes!* to many of these. I believed there were enough to put my plan into practice. I prepared an attractive brochure: Anne's Awesome Arizona Attractions. In question form I listed a large variety of sight-seeing attractions that I felt visitors to Arizona would enjoy seeing. I suggested a number of tour packages. I placed the brochures all over town—in shops, stores, various tourist attractions, motels and travel agencies.

"It started very slowly! At first, just a few at a time, then more and now, referrals from guests who enjoyed our tours keep me busy. In my way, I am satisfied that I am befriending and loving the "alien" visitors to our country. When I have them "captive" in the tour van, I don't preach the Gospel message to them. But each day I pray that they will see Christ in me; and when they do, I am ready to give them a *'reason for the hope that lies within me'"* (I Peter 3:15).[5]

Certainly wisdom and direction of the Holy Spirit will lead you in "entertaining" an international visitor.[6] Though for such a brief time, they are living among us. It is a true privilege to be about our Father's business.

International business people are also in our country, generally for brief periods of time. Possibly ministering Christ's love to them is more suited to your personality. In the next chapter, let's consider how we can *"love them as ourselves"* through His love.

That Hermes was the Greek god of commerce *and* of thieves is "historical" evidence that business behavior and ethical behavior are not always in sync with each other. And with the coming of the New World Order (One World Government), world business and economics are in the media spotlight. We are being made aware of the delicate interrelationships of nations to the survival of civilization. Will Germany emerge above the EU as a superpower to again try to dominate the world? Will China, when they believe they own enough of American real estate, resources and fiat paper, call in their short-term loans? Or, roll them over at a crushingly higher interest rate?

Some countries are deliberately sending their unemployed workers to America. They, in turn, are sending back to their country up to $15 billion annually. In some countries, this accounts for 50% of their gross national product!

While Americans strongly shout for their individual rights, entitlements and what is wrong with the world economy, we are selling the very soul of our nation to the principles of world domination.

On the one hand, for Christians, it is well for us to look up, for our redemption draws closer. After all, we are not of this world system. We are, with Abraham, longing for *"a city whose builder and maker is God"* (Hebrews 11:10). As Paul said to the Christians in Rome, *"...for now our salvation is nearer than when we first believed"* (Romans 13:11b).

But, on the other hand, because we are still in this world, we should look beyond all that this world system is establishing and scan the eternal soul of man that resides in the heart (or liver or throat or spleen, depending on their cultural understanding) of each of the now 7-plus billion beautiful creations of God that people this planet. Most of them are roaming aimlessly, groping for truth and life. But they are not finding it. The latest statistics from the US Center for World Missions say that 3-plus billion people have not even heard the simple message, *"For God so loved the world..."* (John 3:16) in a culturally relevant manner.

International business people of every description and field of endeavor are more and more frequently visiting more and more cities and farms, and even villages in America. They are coming to learn and to trade and to make money. Or, they are coming to teach their American counterpart the technology of their country. Most of them bring with them the emptiness of satan's hopes and America has its red carpet out to help them find fulfillment. "Escort services" fill the pages of every phone directory. A Google search in 0.35 seconds will yield another thousand who will provide, by their advertisement, "every little thing" a lonely business person might want.

Christian, invade this scene with the love of Christ. Embrace these people with the warmth of Christ. Confront them with the claims of Christ. *"Do not take advantage of aliens in your land; do not wrong them. They must be treated like any other citizen; love them as yourself"* (Leviticus 19:33-34).

INFLUENCING THE WORLD'S MILITARY LEADERS FOR CHRIST

Two army officers from the Middle East stood at the altar of a church with their arms raised to heaven. Tears streaming down their faces, each began a simple walk with their new Friend and Savior, Jesus Christ. The path would lead both to a new life, but one to presumed martyrdom.

It happened in San Antonio, Texas.

Every year, military personnel from over 100 nations come to further their training in the United States. Whenever the USA has a defense accord with a country, military personnel from that country can be sent here for specialized training in their fields. San Antonio is a major hub for the training of foreign officers. After English language, medical, or technical training, the officers radiate out to other bases scattered throughout the United States.

A new ministry exists in San Antonio to meet the needs of these souls in uniform. Veteran missionaries David and Jan Hall began the Foreign Armed Forces Network (FAFN) in 2005 to minister to military officers from around the globe. The need in San Antonio was so great that another veteran missionary couple, the Hall's longtime friends Ken and Peggy Krake, joined the work in 2008.

The seed of reaching the military was planted some 20 years before it began to blossom. The Halls were missionaries in Togo at the time. David obtained a press pass to photograph a military parade. As he snapped pictures, he looked into the faces of the men marching by. "My heart was gripped with the need for outreach to the military," said Hall. "Behind the uniforms and the deadpan expressions, I saw faces of real people with a real need of a Savior." He prayed on the spot, "Lord, if you will open this door, I'll walk through it."

Initially, that included distributing 3,000 copies of the New Testament in French to the Togolese military. It would be two decades of prayer before the mission headquarters established a formal policy that foreign militaries should be targeted with the Gospel. The African regional director explained the hesitation. "We tend to be very a-political when we go overseas. Where we have become political, we've done so to our great hurt and discomfort. Any time you get involved too heavily with the military, you're beginning to scratch governmental issues; and in many African countries, you can be military one day and president of the country the next. There are natural concerns which makes you so cautious."

In 2004, the mission gave the Halls permission to establish FAFN, and the initial thought was that they would travel to different countries to minister to international military personnel. After a tough visa situation that refused to resolve, the Halls visited with the Association of Christian Conferences, Teaching and Service (ACCTS—www.accts.org) staff in San Antonio and decided to relocate there.

"I remember the day David Hall called me on my cell phone to tell me about San Antonio," his director commented. "All the lights went on. I thought, 'This is it! It isn't us going to them, it is them coming to us. The world is coming here!' The rest is pure history."

"Six foreign military people came forward two weeks ago, to be saved," noted the pastor of a local church in San Antonio, in a recent interview concerning FAFN. "The impact is incredible. It is measurable. Five of thirteen came up this morning for a salvation call. One officer called me aside after the Halls befriended him and invited him to church. He was leaving the next week. He bowed, and he said, 'I am a man in submission to your God.' I will never forget that experience as long as I live. It took my breath away as I realized what this man in his position was saying."

There have been a number of spectacular conversions such as these, but Hall sees the ministry as a seed planting and watering effort to build relationships and introduce officers to the person of Jesus. Students who come to San Antonio have a reputation for being the future military leadership of their countries. Christians in key positions of leadership can change countries. "Countries normally send their very best people here to study, the ones they look on as having the greatest potential. I heard recently that a student from South Asia that we befriended is now the commander in chief of his nation's armed forces. Only eternity will tell the impact of this ministry," Hall commented.

One African officer came for training in San Antonio disillusioned and said he didn't believe in anything. He attended Bible studies for months. Finally on a Sunday morning before the service, he turned to Hall and said, "There comes a time in a person's life when you have to make a decision. I've made mine, and I want you and the pastor to pray with me after church."

Hall noted that the officer did not go forward for a special appeal or because others were, but because he believed. "He was tall, jet black, slender, a son of the desert. I told him to pray in his native tongue. Then a tear rolled down his cheek. Sometime later, another officer who wasn't at that service, an Eastern Orthodox believer, called me up and asked, 'What happened? He's just blossomed.'"

The Halls and the Krakes also assist ACCTS staff with one Bible study and organize two others. When FAFN began, Echo Company—a company of entry level, raw recruits of foreigners who want to serve in the US army—included a large population of Sudanese Christians who had fled persecution in their homeland. The USAF chaplain assigned to Echo Company at that time requested that FAFN begin English-language Bible studies, open to whoever wished to participate. That Bible study continues to this day. Hall and Krake are also adjunct chaplains at the Air Base Chapel, filling in when too many of the chaplains are deployed.

Not all their work takes place on the base or at church, however. Hospitality accounts for most of FAFN's ministry. The Halls and the Krakes open their homes to the officers and show them around town. They invite them to share holidays and meals together. "We introduce the students to American culture and values. The best way to counter-act the misconceptions about America and Americans is to open your home," explained Krake. "It's about building relationships and taking time. God gives us special moments when we invite students into our homes. The whole world is coming to our doorstep. It's just awesome." Krake's exuberance could not be squelched!

"There was an African officer who had been in our home several times," Krake continued. "When it was time for him to leave San Antonio, I got out of the car to give him a hug, and I could see that he was so afraid he was going to break down and cry. He just turned quickly, and walked away. For him, it was like leaving home. The students are impacted by our openness and the power of God. I saw the glistening in his eyes, and I knew that God had impacted his life and he would never forget that. I could see that when he did his military turn and walked away."

The work has been fruitful, enjoyable and sometimes difficult. "We were used to turnovers in our churches in Europe (serving US military abroad) of one to three years," said Krake. "Here they're changing from two months to a year. One of the great challenges is remembering names and where they are from. You work every angle you can to remember names you've never heard before."

It's also a challenge to serve in an environment where proselytizing is forbidden. "With policy restrictions on proselytizing," said Hall, "my answer is I don't proselytize, I proclaim." We proclaim by lifestyle and word.

"I'm not into putting notches on my pistol grip. The Bible says in John 6:44, *'No one can come to Me unless the Father who sent Me draws him.'* It's the Spirit of God that moves in a person's heart. It's been a liberating experience for me, because it's God who does the work. We are to go into all the world and preach to every nation and make disciples. But God draws them, not us."

The military officers come from all over the world and from all different walks of life, but the largest group of students FAFN ministers to are not Christians. The Halls and the Krakes keep logs of the passengers who ride in their vans. Hall's list is approaching 100 different nationalities. "FAFN is unique and amazing in terms of opportunity," said one mission director, who declined to be named because of the sensitive nature of his work. "I don't know of any other missionaries who have the same kind of opportunity, but anywhere there is a significant population of non-Christian foreigners, the local church can do this. FAFN provides a wonderful model that churches around the country could try. It doesn't have to be military. Every international who lives among us needs a friend."[1]

A friend of mine was in a hotel lobby in New York City on his once-in-a-lifetime trip around the world. In his casual shorts and sports shirt, it was obvious that he had an artificial leg. He was approached by a rather distinguished looking Middle Eastern gentleman who said he also had an artificial limb. Over coffee, they chatted about the world. This man was the Minister of Foreign Affairs for his country. Did he trust in Christ? No. Did he meet a Christian with a sincere interest in him and his country? Yes. At the least, feelings of sincerity and good will were shared. May others water the Seed planted.

And may we rejoice to see the Lord bring forth a soul in His harvest and in the lives this man will influence.

SEAFARERS

Seafarers may not seem like the typical international businessperson, but their contribution to the world economy is clear. The world's seaborne trade totals 8.4 billion tons, annually. It is said that without seafarers, half of the world would starve for lack of transporting food, and the other half would freeze for lack of heating fuel.

Seafarers certainly live in a global village. Ships' crews are made up of a wide variety of nationalities, men *and* women, strangers to each other at the beginning, living aboard together for months on end, often speaking different languages, with different habits and values and of several different religions, or none. Whatever their background, the crew members all have to respect each other's differences and rapidly learn to rely upon one another to do their duty and to keep the ship and themselves safe throughout the voyage. Because of this multi-ethnic mix of people, there is, of course, often a tension on board between the various cultures and traditions. The ship owner or operator must make a commercial profit and run the ship at the lowest cost, and so will recruit from the most economic labor supply.

Crew contracts generally call for ten months or more of service at modest rates and few benefits. For those ten months, the seafarer works and lives in virtual isolation in the middle of the ocean. For the brief time that the ship is in port, the seafarer is regarded as a security risk and often denied shore leave. In those ten months, he will miss his family desperately. He will have no television or daily newspaper. He'll run out of toothpaste and other necessities, and he will barely have opportunity to shop, to see the dentist or even to call home.

Ministry opportunity to this group of internationals living among us is limited to the ports of call on our coasts and around the Great Lakes. Advocating for them to have shore leave to go shopping, to see a doctor or dentist, or just to stand on solid ground may seem like less than valuable. But those organizations which have Port Chaplains tell otherwise. Just to listen to their stories of hopes and fears and concerns that they have is time to build relationships. Seafarers are real people no less valuable than ourselves, in need of compassionate care and in need of a Savior. You could even introduce them to your Friend who walked on water and calmed the stormy sea.[2]

Listen to Dianne Boyce's excitement as God has given her a vision for one group of seafarers:

My heart is eager to return this summer to the Bergen Seaman's Mission where we will provide a "home away from home" for the crew members of cruise ships coming in to Bergen. Over 300 ships arrive there between May and September. Those who work on the ships live a hard life, often working 12 to 14 hours a day, seven days a week. Their quarters are small as is their pay. They miss their families and are eager to contact them by Internet and Skype whenever they can. Internet on board the ship is too expensive for most crew to use. At the Mission we provide free Internet. Phone cards and phones are also available.

We make the mission as comfortable and homey as possible. Each morning we bake Norwegian waffles for them, and keep the coffee and tea ready. Everything is free.

Since the crews come from many different nations, it is nice to have games where language is not an issue, so we keep Chess and Jenga available to play. It gives us opportunity to build a relationship with them even with our limited vocabulary. Love is a universal language! Last year we started a Bible Study/Prayer time in the afternoon. The crewmembers were a bit shy to come at first, but soon the small room was filled with men and women very attentive and hungry for the Word of God. As you can imagine, there are many temptations aboard the ship. Morality is low. Fidelity is in danger because of loneliness and homesickness. Counsel and prayer are often requested, and we have the joy of sharing the forgiveness provided in the cross of Christ, as well as His abiding strength through the Holy Spirit. When they are ready to return to their ship, we offer each one a CD with the Gospel message in his or her native language as a parting gift.

There are two experiences I would like to share with you. The first is about Victor, a young Filipino who had recently lost his mother. He was heartbroken. I prayed with him and we cried together. I talked with him about Jesus' love and forgiveness. He was so close to receiving his Savior but was not yet ready. I promised to pray for him and keep in touch. We still visit on Facebook even after four years. I care for him like a son, and trust that the time will come when he will yield his life to the Lord.

The second story is about a young Vietnamese woman—for her safety I will not mention her name. She was very sad and discouraged. She had a big dream for her life, but was unable to realize it in her present circumstances. She was Muslim and it was Ramadan, so she was fasting during the day. I asked if I might pray with her.

She said, "Yes." I said, "I am a Christian. I will pray in the name of Jesus. Are you okay with that?" She again said, "Yes." I prayed that God would fulfill the dream of her heart. I believe He will, and she will know that He is God. After we prayed, I gave her a small New Testament and told her when she needed comfort she should read it. She gladly received it. I trust that through the power of God's Word she will come to know Him!

I leave in a week. I can hardly wait to be there; to light the candles on the tables, arrange fresh flowers, and be waiting at the door to say, "Welcome! Good morning, we're so glad you've come! This is your home away from home."[3]

Dianne does not live in a port city, so she went to a port city to minister Christ's love and forgiveness. Apply your own creativity for ideas to minister to the internationals who live among us.

CULTURAL DISTINCTIVES

To work with internationals who live among us is exciting and challenging. There is so much to learn. Beyond knowing a few general principles, learning on-the-job is probably the best way to discover what makes us different. Yet, we need to always keep in mind the one thing that unites them: They were created by God to worship Him; they are in need of the Savior.

Different cultures have different rules. Cultural distinctives are not necessarily good or bad, just different. Sometimes we don't know what the rules are until one is broken. Welcome to the ambiguity of cross-cultural ministry!

As more and more internationals come to live among us—whether for a short business trip or as permanent residents—ignoring these rules can cause misunderstandings and conflict. But by developing sensitivity to them and accepting the challenge to learn them, we can get past those barriers to the individuals behind them. Since it is the individual for whom Christ died, not the culture, we need to bridge the gaps in relationships that these cultural distinctives create.

The nuances of culture are as varied as the shades and hues of color that are in the rainbow, so there is no encyclopedia to study for the answers. Rather, relationships will be built by watching and listening and talking with internationals. But to get a general idea of the areas of life in which these distinctives occur, we would like to look at a few examples.

Eye Contact: The average American makes eye contact with friends or acquaintances for about one or two seconds at a time. This contrasts strongly with many people in the Middle East or France who might gaze for long periods during conversation, hoping to create a bond of communication. The Asian culture, however, teaches that it is rude to stare directly at the person with whom they are talking. Thus, often you will find them wanting to stand next to you—looking with you at some distant object.

Personal Space: Each culture defines what is the comfortable speaking distance between people. A Hispanic man may touch his companion's arm or even hold the person's coat lapel while conversing. An Asian may prefer to stand two or three feet away, while someone from the Middle East might stand just a foot away from a companion of the same sex.

An interesting exercise in humor is to stand in the foyer of your church and watch two people of varying personal space "dance" around the room. The one who enjoys a greater space backs away; the one who prefers a close distance moves closer. Around the room they go—one advancing, the other retreating!

Public Recognition: Americans traditionally love a "pat on the back," (not Christians, of course!) and it is even more appreciated if it is done in the public arena for all to hear. Many other cultures, however, find individual acknowledgment embarrassing; it is the success of the group that matters the most. Thus: An elder from the very first Christian church in Mongolia addressed a congregation in California. At the conclusion, the audience gave him a standing ovation. What could he do but clap his hands along with them.

Holidays: With the commercialization of Christmas, the season itself has extreme cultural variables, creating massive misunderstandings. Some Southeast Asian people, having heard that Christmas is a time for Santa Claus and business profits and mangers and stars, made a shop display with Santa Claus in the manger of hay.

In Italy, one group of churches likes to center their displays around the crèche, despising as pagan, any recognition of the Christmas tree. Whereas, the Christmas tree folk despise the crèche. Other Christians believe neither should have a place in celebrating Christmas.

We have our printing done by a Middle Easterner. In a festive Christmas spirit, having received a Christmas card and calendar from him, one day when I was there, I wished him a 'Merry Christmas!' Whoops! Back peddle! I was grasping at the air, trying to pull those words back into my mouth! He was culturally sensitive to me (in sending me the card), but I offended his culture by saying my 'Merry Christmas' to him! Actually, it turned out okay as, with an apology for my blunder, it gave another opportunity to talk with him about my belief in Jesus and in his need for a Savior.

Accents: Judging a person by his accent or ability to speak English can lead to some misunderstandings. Some languages have very different roots. Many of the sounds in English are not easily heard, thus difficult to pronounce. In fact, English is considered one of the three most difficult languages to learn as a second language. (The other two are Chinese and Navajo.) That should put things in perspective and increase our tolerance for our international guests.

Colloquialisms: From Groovy to Cool; from rad to bad; from Hippie to Yuppie to GenX to Millennial. It is hard enough for us to keep up with the "in" and "out" words of our own culture...and then we wonder if "in" and "out" are in or out! I once found myself being called "sand" because I had not kept up on youth jargon!

Bring in Herr German Businessman who has carefully practiced the precise grammatical structure and pronunciation of the "King's English" only to meet some Groovy Cat from Silicon Valley, who, hiding behind his Oakley reflective sunglasses, asks the dude what his addy is! I think you get the picture.

At the close of a business session, one may say, "I will call you." If he doesn't, the prospective business associate does not sue him for breach of contract; he realizes it was just a polite way of saying, "I don't think I will be doing business with you."

At the close of a meal we enjoyed at the home of the aunt and uncle of our Peruvian friend (he had told them about us and they wanted to meet us), we were saying all of the nice leave-taking phrases, one of which was, "You will have to come to our house for dinner." Before we could move on to further light, noncommittal words, we were ushered to their wall calendar for a date! "Would this next Sunday be okay?" they asked.

Lesson learned! Our door is now *always* open for guests!

Communication Styles: Some cultures habitually soften requests by adding a lot of words, such as, "If it would not be too much trouble, I would really appreciate it if I could have a cup of coffee." In other cultures, when the request is streamlined, "Get me some coffee" can sound like an order and appear rude and pushy. And if you just said to yourself, "Well, it *is* rude," you can understand a source of misunderstanding when cultures meet.

Time: Americans are known for wanting to get to the bottom line right away. With Mexicans, Japanese or Near Easterners, getting to know an individual is often essential before talking business.

A team of African businessmen had been offended in the opening round of talks with their American counterparts. They spent the night discussing among themselves how to lay a strategy that would ultimately result in a forced apology from the Americans.

In the morning, at the first sign of awareness that an offense had been committed, the Americans immediately and profusely apologized. The rest of the morning they just went round and round in debate. Just before lunch, the meeting ended in good spirits. Later, an American asked why it had been so difficult to straighten out such a small matter. The answer he received was an education in cultural sensitivity: "You made the mistake of apologizing too quickly. You should have held forth your innocence so we could talk out the case we had spent the night building against you. We were denied the opportunity of forcing an admission, so we just talked on and on, even though there was nothing more to say."

A missionary candidate was attending our ACTS 29 Training Course in Tijuana, Mexico. The adult son of his host family worked at a VW repair garage. The candidate's interest in cars and his requirement to spend time in the culture had him stop by one day. The worker wiped the grease off his hands and sat down to talk. After a few minutes our student said, "Isn't that the boss over there? Don't you need to get back to work?" Answer: "No. It's okay. My dad told me about you. I've been wanting to meet you." They talked on for half an hour! At class the next day, it was still a puzzle to him that relationships in that culture were more important than production.[4]

I am sure that by this time you can add your own story. Relating with internationals brings out the nuances of cultural distinctives. Our goal is to listen and learn—to get past the variables of culture to be able to say, "You must be born again!" Whoops! Do not say that to a Hindu from India. He will think, "How great! They also believe in reincarnation!"

A VISITING RESEARCH PROFESSOR

It was my privilege to interview Doctor Hirokisa Morikawa the day before his return to Japan. We met in his home, and yes, my shoes came off at the door. Thank God I had un-holey socks on! Everything was in various stages of being packed or discarded. Evidently cooking utensils were packed or returned, for there were the telltale signs of fast food meals. "Please excuse my wife," he requested, as she was out doing some last minute errands.

Doctor Morikawa had been here for eight months as a visiting research professor. He was in San Diego on a scholarship by the Ministry of Education of Japan to do research in biomechanics at the University of California, San Diego (UCSD). Meet Doctor Morikawa:

Neal Pirolo: Doctor Hiro (for this is what he asked me to call him), thank you for graciously receiving me at this busy time. But as you are leaving so soon, maybe this is the best time for you to give your reflections on your visit to the States.

Dr. Hiro: I was happy to meet you at church on Sunday and to spend this time with you now.

NP: Dr. Hiro, was this your first stay in America, or have you been here before?

Dr. Hiro: About seven years ago I was in California on a church visitation tour of the Los Angeles area. We visited a number of good churches. At one, each morning we had classes on theology, United States culture, and how American people and Christians think about the cults.

NP: Did those classes take up your whole time?

Dr. Hiro: No. Another of the cooperating churches had planned several sight seeing tours. Biola University also helped organize our visit. It was at that time that I heard about Calvary Chapel of Costa Mesa—that they were solid in teaching the Word and were free in the Spirit. I knew I wanted to learn how to touch that free Spirit for our churches back home.

NP: Were you able to visit that church?

Dr. Hiro: No. Time and lack of transportation did not allow it.

NP: Research in biomechanics sounds...so technical. Can you explain simply what you were doing at UCSD?

Dr. Hiro: The specific area of biomechanics research we were conducting had to do with the flow of blood through artificial blood vessels. When these devices build up with cholesterol and other obstacles, the blood flow is severely restricted. We were experimenting with vessels made of hydrogel. The area of real difficulty is getting the artificial vessel to interact with the real blood vessel. The red blood cells have a lot to do with this interaction. Hydrogel seems to be an answer.

NP: Doctor Hiro, I thought the common practice of using a vein from the person's leg provided good material for replacing the clogged vessels around the heart.

Dr. Hiro: Not really. The mechanical characteristics of veins are weaker than arteries. The realization of this fact was the beginning of my interest in this research. I had been studying the external flow of fish movement. It is very similar to the internal flow of blood vessels.

NP: Well, are you going home satisfied with your research?

Dr. Hiro: We have made some good progress.

> I interrupt this interview to address an expressed issue that America is being robbed of her brain trust. "All of the development of our technology is being siphoned off and applied to the development of products by other nations, who then reap the profits," is shouted from many quarters.
>
> Did you begin to identify with the feelings generated by that expressed concern? Did you say or think, "Yes, they come here and learn all that they can, then go back to their country and reap the benefits?" If yes, it shows how easily we can get caught up in the "flesh and blood" economic battles of this world. And to the degree that these battles dissipate our physical, emotional, mental and spiritual energy, to that degree we are at a loss to fight the real enemy—satan. Paul said it so simply: *"For we wrestle not against flesh and blood..."* (Ephesians 6:12) May we focus all our energy on the real battle—the battle for lost souls.

NP: How is it that you came to Maranatha Chapel?

Dr. Hiro: A Japanese pastor who was doing some work at Biola University gave me a list of churches in the San Diego area. The first one on the list was Maranatha Chapel. On our first Sunday we were met by the wife of a doctor. The next Sunday she introduced us to her husband, Doctor T.V. Varughese, as the director of the International Home Fellowship. He was very friendly and helpful. We thought it would be a good idea to meet other internationals, and a good opportunity to study the Bible.

NP: You were still looking for that "strong in the Word, free in the Spirit" you had heard about. Is that right?

Dr. Hiro: Yes, Japan and other Asian nations do not have the spiritual or even the cultural basis of Christianity. Rather, Buddhism and Confucianism dominate. This makes outreach back home very limited. Let me enlarge: In Japan, centuries ago, Buddhism and Shinto were in conflict because they were logically incompatible. An ancient Buddhist teacher came up with the idea that the two religions belong to "different realms of truth." So any apparent contradiction between them is an illusion. Thus began postmodern thought in Japan, before the rest of the world even made it to modernism. The ramifications for today are that Japanese are raised in a system of double-think. They can look at two contradictory truth claims and hold them both at the same time, if those "truths" are in the realm of the spiritual. When faith is relegated to religious thought that doesn't need to be true in the same way as historical truth, it becomes very difficult for people to come to Christ. Of course, relativity is also now finding its way into historical truth.

NP: That is valuable insight in relating with Japanese here or in Japan. I know the Bible has been in the Japanese language for generations. Are there not good study or inspirational books to help people of your country?

Dr. Hiro: There are books that have been translated into Japanese but they cannot be used easily because they are not culturally relevant. But at Dr. T.V.'s Bible study, we were introduced to a study he prepared, called *Evangelistic Bible Course for Internationals.*[5] Dr. T.V., being an international himself from India, knows how to speak to internationals. It is very good. The church is so large, it is fortunate for us to have been introduced to Dr. T.V.

NP: What if you had not met him?

Dr. Hiro: I saw the listings of home fellowships, but I had no idea what they were and I would not have called to find out. If a person were aggressive, possibly...but as for us, we probably would not have. Also, if one can speak English well, one might be more forward to reach out. The atmosphere at Maranatha Chapel is great. The focus is bright in message and songs. Maybe if there were visitor cards for newcomers. But we have the same problem in Japan. When a church grows bigger and bigger, they have no systematic plan to follow up on new people. It is good that the church provides a song sheet for foreigners.

NP: Outside of church, did you have many contacts?

Dr. Hiro: We met many medical doctors at UCSD and in the lab—many from China. The Professor Emeritus, head of the Department of Applied Medicine and Engineering Science was Chinese. It was very difficult to talk with any of them about the Gospel, but I had a lot of opportunity to discuss creation/evolution. We brought several couples to Maranatha Chapel and to Dr. T.V.'s home fellowship. They told us the atmosphere at the church was great, but they could not understand the English. So they went to a Japanese-speaking church. They loved the songs—the spirit of freedom and life—but they struggled with the English.

NP: If the church had provided lessons in ESL, would that have helped?

Dr. Hiro: Yes, I am sure some would have taken advantage of that. But we were all on a very busy schedule and our stay was so short. Through the community college we could have gotten help. Also, UCSD has an Intercultural Center that would have provided a tutor—at a cost. Having an ESL program in a church environment would have been very good.

NP: Why did you continue at Maranatha Chapel since there are Japanese-speaking churches in San Diego?

Dr. Hiro: Some Japanese like to go to a Japanese church, but we wanted to know how Christianity is applied to life. The Japanese separate the life of business and the life of church. That dichotomy is deeply rooted in our history, as I was saying before. And our interest is to communicate and relate with internationals. Maranatha Chapel emphasized being born again. Many Japanese churches do not emphasize the Word and freedom in the Spirit, so their lives are not a good testimony of the joy of the Lord. They are still bound. In fact, less than one percent of the population of Japan has any form of Christianity.

NP: Were you able to relate with any other people during your stay in San Diego?

Dr. Hiro: The UCSD Intercultural Center introduced us to a Navy couple—a Commander who had signed up for the friendship program. We would meet every month—first at our home, then at theirs. They took us out to the desert and Universal Studios. We had a tour of an aircraft carrier. We enjoyed relating with internationals. There are certainly a lot of differences between cultures.

NP: What are some of those differences that you struggled with?

Dr. Hiro: It was hard to call people by their first names. After I got accustomed to the idea, it was okay. I still bow to the Chinese! But to the Americans, I raise my hand and say, "Hi!" We never put our hands in our pockets when we talk. Many other little things. I cannot remember them all just now.

NP: I'm sorry! All this time you have been letting me call you by your first name! Professor Doctor Hirokisa Morikawa, you have seemed pretty happy with your experience here. Did nothing bad happen?

Dr. Hiro: Really, that's okay! I realize my name is difficult for an English speaker. The only trouble we had was when we bought a used car. There were problems two times within the first month. They fixed them because there was a 30-day warranty. But I worried. Yes, it broke again—after the warranty. It cost $1000 to fix it! But everything else has been excellent. God has led us and blessed us.[6]

THE BOTTOM LINE

In the business world, we like the "bottom line." We can enjoy reading about what others are doing in a particular area of involvement. To a degree we can vicariously identify with that action, but it is quite another thing to allow their actions to give us insight and motivate us to action.

At this critical point our own motivation can take us in any number of directions. See if you find your reaction to these interviews and stories in the following list:

1) To rejoice in the Lord that someone is relating with international business people;
2) To feel "warm" because *they* are doing it and not *me*;
3) To let the fact that they are doing it immunize my conscience from taking action;
4) To confirm that that which I am doing in His Kingdom work is right for me;
5) To challenge me to take some related action;
6) To think of someone I know who would like to use these ideas to expand their creative involvement with internationals who live among us.

From conducting these interviews, doing research and writing this chapter, I can summarize the following ideas for your considered use. I'm sure you can add more of your own!

- Airport hospitality for arriving internationals—a "welcome" basket from your church or a civic organization...
- Offer English, American culture and other classes at your church...
- Interview internationals and publish them to promote better understanding...
- Contact David Hall[7] to see if any of those military personnel have been assigned to your city...
- Hospitality: housing, vehicle, license, insurance, shopping...
- Invite them to your house for dinner...
- Volunteer for the friendship programs at colleges and corporations...
- Establish a USA (or regional) tour company catering to internationals...
- Contact such organizations as the Christian Businessmen's Committee or the Christian Business Association for ideas of ministering among these internationals...

Now, add your own ideas and minister in Jesus' Name!

The challenges of cross-cultural ministry in our own country may seem strange, or awkward. You may have been taught that missions is us going "over there." As you read about these internationals who live among us, I trust you are asking God for His counsel and direction for your involvement.

If business people do not seem to be a "good fit," consider an equally challenging group of internationals in the next chapter.

IF I WERE A REFUGEE

If I were a refugee, I would arise from my straw mat in the pitch black of another cold and dreary rainy-season morning. It is 4:00 A.M. The rooster crowing is not mine. It would take a month's hard-earned wages to buy one. Besides, I have to save for a new pair of glasses to replace the ones stolen from my tiny mud hut three months ago.

If I were a refugee, I would grab a small piece of dried cornmeal mush on my way out the door. It will be my only meal until I return home in about 14 hours. I push the plastic curtains aside as I step into another day. The first gray of dawn illuminates the sprawling refugee camp that has been my home for more than three years. Already a few women are making their way to the well for water, trying to beat the early morning rush when dozens of women will line up, sometimes waiting for hours for their turn.

If I were a refugee, I would try to stretch away the aches of a restless night's sleep. I glance across the river to the shadowy features on the other side where my homeland lies in darkness still.

If I were a refugee, I would begin the 10-mile walk to where firewood is gathered. In about four hours, I climb a ridge and descend part way down the other side to a small forest of eucalyptus and acacia. The trees along the riverbank and around the refugee camp have long since disappeared, cut down to fuel the more than 15,000 cooking fires of our camp. I look at the closest tree. I am already exhausted from this daily trek, but if

I sit down to rest, I will not want to get back up. I bite a small portion of the hardened mush and begin hacking one of the tree branches with my machete.

If I were a refugee, I would try to focus on chopping, but the horrors and memories of that day keep replaying the nightmares of our escape. I was a farmer in my homeland. One day while my wife and I were working in the field, an air attack hit our village. "The children," I cried. We ran toward the village, where the dry thatch roofed huts of mine and our friends' exploded in flames. Bombs burst around us as we ran toward our home. It was in flames. Everything we had worked for—gone in that instant. We spotted our four children running aimlessly, this way and that, not knowing where to go. Their screams for help still echo in my ears. We quickly rounded them up and ran for cover. We took refuge in a nearby forest.

If I were a refugee, after three hours of relentless bombing, I would return to the village clearing. The village is pitted, scorched and deathly silent. My cousin had evidently thought there would be safety in his hut. His lifeless body is sprawled in the doorway. We bury him in a hastily dug grave, and with my family make our way across the river border at night to avoid detection by the rebels. We learn that we are six of nearly half a million who cross the border of our country to seek refuge. Our camp has about 50,000 people. We're called "refugees." But we are people with names and hopes and fears. We fight malaria, poor sanitation and overcrowding. And we wait for peace in our homeland.

If I were a refugee, I would pass my days inside our one-room "apartment." I dare not venture out in the daytime. I would be suspected of looking for work, taking a job away from the nationals. I would like to work—to learn a trade, but I can't read or write. Yes, I learned my mother's language, but I can also speak the language of our "temporary" home. You see, I was born here. My parents were fleeing the horrors of feuding tribes. My father was shot in the back just as they were rushing the border. My mother was raped by two or three of the rebels before they threw her in the river bordering our countries.

If I were a refugee, I would try to believe my mother when she tells me that she was already pregnant by her husband, but I will never know who my father is. I am now 15. From time to time, workers come from other countries and try to teach us. They are encouraged that I have a desire to learn and I have learned a bit of English and math. My mother has long since given up telling me stories of our homeland. Her hopes of returning have dimmed. As she sees my features developing, I think she, too, realizes that I am a son of a rebel!

If I were a refugee, I would again make the trek to the clinic at the other end of the camp. My baby, Esther, is sick. I wait my turn for a nurse to give me some medicine. I look around at the pale green walls lined with chairs. Mothers with eyes as hollow as mine, also wait, hoping they will be called before the medicine runs out. I try not to think about it, but in the emptiness of anything positive, those thoughts return again and again. My husband was a strongly opinionated man. He saw a cause he thought was worth fighting for. I tried to stop him, but I knew better. His warring spirit was overpowering.

As his wife, I was in danger. I had no choice but to flee. I left our house with nothing but our two children, three-year-old Hannah and my baby, Esther. With over 40,000 refugees in this settlement camp, services are not enough. Sanitation and hygiene are poor, so the incidence of diarrhea among children is high. The thought stalks my heart. I relive the horror of bringing my three year old to sit in this same chair last month. The nurse took her frail body wracked with fever and dehydration. She shook her head, hopelessly. I took her home to die.

As I hear my name called, my mind snaps back to the present. I look down at the peaceful face of my baby. I stand and say to the nurse, "You can give the medicine to the next mother." My Esther is dead in my arms.

If I were a refugee, I would have already travelled about 350 kilometers from a transit camp to this more permanent "home"—a resettlement camp while we wait for the fighting to stop in our homeland. My parents did not want to leave the transit camp because leaving took us further from home. My father feared we would never be able to return but nothing can be done about that now.

I don't know how it happened, but in the loading of the buses, my sister and I were separated from our parents. We strained to look out the back window to see them. Yes, it looked like they were in the next bus but we never saw them again. We were processed into this camp of 800,000 people, with hundreds arriving each day. We don't know how to look for our parents. I am sure they are looking for us. It has been a year now. I am sixteen. I don't want to say this, but I have resorted to selling my body in order to provide for my thirteen-year-old sister and myself. I send her outside when the men come, but I am sure she knows what is happening. The other day I heard someone say the word, HIV. I thought it might be one of those social organizations that come to help. I am too embarrassed to ask. I hope our parents find us.[1]

If I were a refugee...!

Twenty-two years ago, I wrote a series of essays on refugees. Today, in doing my research—reading story after story of the plight that plagues these people and the meager effort being put forth to help, I realized I could have used the same writing by merely changing the country names, and by increasing the statistical figures. And yet, the numbers continue to rise. In some cases, the names do not need changing. The sad saga continues. And the faces of the people have the same blank stare of hopelessness.

1991: "Incredible pressure is being put on the Nicaraguan refugees to return to their homeland. But they fear for their lives and the lives of their children and loved ones. At the same time, survival in Honduras is becoming increasingly difficult."

2013: "Today the team went to a very poor village called Guarari. It is an area solely dedicated (unofficially) for Nicaraguan refugees. These refugees are in Costa Rica illegally and do not have any status or ability to receive any government assistance. The housing is basically tin shacks with sewage running through the middle of the main street. This sewer is an open stream. The outhouses are perched on the banks of it. A bridge over the sewer connects the two halves of this refugee camp. Due to their status, the living conditions are difficult. With poverty and without proper housing or medical treatment, and continual exposure to drugs from dealers from without and from within their own family, the youth are pressured to fend for themselves."[2]

1991: "After a 13-month cease-fire, Tamil separatists resumed a 7-year old war with the Sri Lankan government. Refugees tell horror stories of mass shootings and machete massacres of innocent civilians. In one incident 30 pregnant women were lined up and shot by Sinhalese soldiers. Since the war resumed, 50,000 Tamil refugees have escaped from Sri Lanka, crossing the 30-mile stretch of sea to the southern tip of India."

2013: "About 72,000 Tamil refugees remain in camps funded and run by the Indian government in the southern state of Tamil Nadu. In comparison to the brutal days of Sri Lanka's civil war, life is good in the camps. Residents have access to education and health services identical to their Indian neighbors outside of the wire fence. But there is little hope. The refugees scrap for the lowest-paying, most dangerous jobs—those the locals won't take. All of the children and teenagers were born in India. Yet, they can never become Indian citizens nor can they return to their parents' homeland. The frustration level is greatly heightened—*unbearably so*—by the prospect of an entire life spent as a refugee."[3]

News items appear from time to time saying the governments of the two countries are making progress in developing a means for allowing the refugees to return to Sri Lanka. But...they wait and hope and...!

In a tragic comedy, countries that were hosting refugees ten years ago are now at war. People from those hosting countries are now fleeing to the once warring country for safety! In what might be the ultimate irony in refugee migration, there are Sudanese fleeing into Ethiopia while at the same time some Ethiopians are seeking refuge in Sudan. The statistics of the maddening genocide in Darfur defy all reason. Even with the dividing of the country, war continues. The refugees continue to flee.

A Google search will give you current statistics, but as of this writing refugees in Somalia are pouring into Dadaab, already the largest refugee camp in the world with over 800,000 souls.

The new wave of refugees fleeing the conflict in Mali is swelling the population in some border villages of Niger from 1000 to 7000 or more. For people who were already living at subsistence levels, there is no way for them to absorb these new arrivals. Yet, they keep coming.

In the Kala Refugee Camp, Zambia's largest, Congolese face the challenge of protecting their children from malnutrition and infection from malaria—both potentially fatal. "Sometimes we just stay hungry. In a month there are about six days when we don't eat anything," one mother states blankly. Yet, they keep coming.

Thousands are fleeing the violence in the Democratic Republic of Congo and ending up in refugee camps in Uganda. Most are under the age of 15. They have fled in fear of being forcibly recruited into armed rival groups. Ugandan refugees are being displaced from the terror of Northern Uganda. Yet, they keep coming.

More then four million Iraqis have been forced by violence, threats, kidnapping and instability to flee their houses. Ongoing violence in Syria has led to a growing refugee population in Jordan and Lebanon. Lebanon was already struggling with the Palestinian refugees (actually the grandchildren of the 1948-49 war with Israel). These people for whom Christ died have no rights or opportunity for education outside of their camps. Hatred is the foundation for anything that they might learn inside the camps. Yet, they keep coming.

Yet, they keep coming!

WHO IS A REFUGEE?

According to the 1951 United Nations Geneva Convention on Refugees, a refugee is "any person who, owing to well-founded fear of being persecuted for reason of race, religion, nationality or political opinion, is outside the country of his nationality and is unable or, owing to such fear for reasons other than personal convenience, is unwilling to avail himself of the protection of the country; or, who, not having a nationality and being outside the country of his former habitual residence, is unable or, owing to such fear or for reasons other than personal convenience, is unwilling to return to it."[4]

WHY DON'T THEY JUST GO HOME?

There is no single, simple answer. Rains in Bangladesh and drought in Ethiopia do wreck havoc. But natural disasters are not what push most refugees out of their homes. Escape from the violence of man-made struggles is paramount. The primary causes of refugee migration are armed conflict back home, gross human rights violations and/or well-founded fear of ethnic, religious or political persecution.

The war is "over." Why don't they just go home? Reuniting large refugee populations with their native country is not so easily accomplished as just to say, "Go home now!" The challenge lies in at least six areas:

1) "I have an uncle who made it to the United States, and I want to go there to live. In America I can get an education and make money. Neither of these options would be available to me if I return to my home country."

2) "The war is 'over?' Though a cease-fire has been signed on paper, bloodshed continues as sides are taken. The hatred of peoples does not end with the signing of a paper. Real statistics indicate that people are still leaving my homeland."

3) In addition to continued fighting, there are other lingering, deadly deterrents to the long march home: leftover munitions of war—unexploded shells and land mines. Those who are returning either send herds of goats or use their bare hands, groping inch by inch across former battlefields. Some have sent their children to detonate the land mines! Hospitals are filled with mine victims.

4) Another troubling cloud on the horizon is how the refugees will feed themselves once they return. Fertile plains and valleys may have remained fallow for years. The transportation systems are virtually nonexistent and much of the livestock

has been lost in the fighting. Everything will have to be rebuilt from the foundation up. The resources for rebuilding largely have been destroyed.

5) Many refugees also face a psychological deterrent. They do not want to return. "Ten years as a refugee can have a profound impact on a person. Life in a refugee camp may not be the most comfortable situation, but it may be 'light years' ahead of life in his home country," commented a U.N. worker. One refugee, having lived in one camp for three years and now in a warehouse in Macau for seven said, "I would do it all over again. What I am experiencing here is far better than the prospects of returning home."

6) The social structure of the refugee has also changed during his refuge in a camp. Many refugees, now in their late teens, remember little of their homeland after ten years. And they speak with scant regard for the traditional ways they may be subject to once back in their homeland.[5]

Though hundreds of thousands of Afghan refugees have returned home, the majority of the 2.7 million registered Afghans still living in Pakistan and Iran have lived in exile for over two and a half decades. More than half that number was born abroad and as a result they face more complex reintegration challenges than their compatriots who left Afghanistan more recently.

These are all aspects of the future that each refugee must wonder and consider. Only a small percentage of all refugees return to their home country.

WHY DON'T THEY GO TO A NEW COUNTRY?

While just over one percent return home, another one percent are able to relocate in a new country. Nearly ninety-eight percent of all refugees remain in squalid "resettlement" camps—a lifelong road to nowhere! Why can't they just...get up and go? Why can't they make a new start in a new country?

First, some authorities voice concern that race (color) may play a major part. After World War II, there were 10 million refugees, mostly white, and within a decade most of them were either home or resettled in a new country. Today's refugees, on the other hand, are mostly black, golden or brown.

The typical refugee profile is no longer that of a white European fleeing communism. The geographical origin has moved from the northern countries to those south and the reasons for flight are not as popularly understood as "escape from communism." In most cases those fleeing today are bringing their religious and political beliefs with them even as they flee from violence or deprivation or persecution from their political left or right. The multiple shades of color of today's dilemma are not as easily distinguishable as "white fleeing red." Arms do not quickly open to receive people so different from me!

Selective asylum is a second factor in this knotty issue of relocation. Refugees from several countries could be fleeing from similar circumstances. However, the U.S. government grants asylum on a very unequal basis. The rapid assimilation of "desirables" and the equally quick deportation of those the government rejects as "undesirables" adds to the problem.

Third, as the wall of protectivism through floodlights, border guards and vigilante squads try to stem the flow of illegals from our southern border, another problem of gigantic proportion arises. A family "makes it to the border." There is only enough money for Papa to cross. "I'll make plenty of money and send for you soon," he assures his wife and children. He never returns; nor does his money. Mother makes her move, leaving her children with friends she has made. She never returns.

The "friends" can no longer care for her children. They are turned out into the street to join the more than 200,000 child "refugees" under the age of twelve who roam the ghettos of Tijuana, Baja Mexico!

Fourth, beyond the issues of restrictive policies of host countries, a new question is rising: Will there be enough money to care for the world's refugee population? In 1951 the United Nations created the High Commission for Refugees (UNHCR) to assist Europeans after WWII. It was to exist for only three years—just long enough to settle the war's refugees and displaced persons.

More than 60 years later, straining under budget cuts and rising costs to care for an ever-increasing population, and despite all efforts to trim programs to their bare minimum, cutbacks are threatening the UNHCR's ability to carry out its most basic responsibilities and puts the lives of millions of refugees at risk.

A fifth factor—and I believe this is most basic, even possibly encompassing the other four—is the dilemma called compassion fatigue. The countries of the world capable of receiving relocating refugees are simply growing weary of being bombarded with images of gaunt, miserable-looking individuals of strange lands living in tent cities.

Compassion fatigue is a contemporary sickness. The symptoms are an initial rush of concern for a distant and obviously suffering group. Time and the press of other priorities push the thoughts of refugees into the recesses of memory. When the pictures again and again show up as margin advertisements on the computer screen, conscience may be pricked for a moment. However, the repeated images can produce tedium and a feeling of withdrawal that sometimes descends to disdain. Those who suffer from compassion fatigue are compelled to first express and then deny any sympathy. Thus, today's cause becomes tomorrow's bore. (How many "causes" can we read about on the social networks today before we, too, become fatigued?) Refugees and disaster are like fashions. They change rapidly. Images and their accompanying statistics that command our attention this week are cast aside impatiently next week.

But refugees are NOT statistics! They are men and women, boys and girls, many of whom have never seen what's on the other side of that 15-foot high block wall, topped with some spiral of barbed wire.

All that has been written to this point is to emphasize the desperate needs of these people for whom Christ died. Now, Christian, we can expend our energy debating the social justice issues that definitely do cloud the problems refugees and their host nations face. *Or,* we can respond in Jesus' words, *"I was a stranger and you took Me in"* (Matt 25:35).

WHAT CAN WE DO ABOUT IT?

It is 10:30 a.m. The Cathay Pacific jet noses its way into its berth at the Los Angeles International Airport. The gyros and other electronic gear whine down to silence. The gigantic metal tube disgorges its captain, crew and 284 passengers, including 73 unbearably excited refugees.

One by one, they step in front of the passport worker's booth and then up to the desk of the Immigration and Naturalization Service (INS) official for fingerprinting, photo-taking and more stamps. They carry their things to the Department of Agriculture inspector: an old cassette tape player (now unusable, though they don't know that yet), a jar of noodles soaked in vinegar, bath slippers. The noodles stay; they are free to go! They are free!

Other planes from far away places land today in equally busy airports around America giving one of the most destitute groups of humanity a "second chance" at "life, liberty and the pursuit of happiness."

Less than 150 miles to the south of LAX, at the INS checkpoint in San Diego, thousands of Mexican and other Latin Americans are waved through the border each month. Many more, perhaps 50 times the legal arrivals, slip quietly over that invisible line in the sand. (Read again, Chapter Four, to consider what you might be able to do for those internationals who live among us.) More than 2 million refugees have arrived in the United States since the Refugee Act of 1980 was established, driven from their homelands by war, political change, and social, religious, and ethnic oppression. These flows were marked first by refugees primarily from Southeast Asia and the Soviet Union in the 1970s and 1980s during the Cold War period, followed by Europe in the 1990s during the Balkans period, and a growing number from Africa in the 2000s during the civil conflict period. In the second decade of the Twenty-first Century, add to those numbers the thousands being brought in from the Middle Eastern countries.

Cluster sites across America have brought a patchwork of internationals that—when the figures are known—everybody is a member of a minority! And the floodgates don't seem to be closing. Every president and Congress promises to "do something" about the staggering numbers of people this immigration issue represents.

The international hordes of refugees now streaming in from the east, west, north and south embody dreams and hopes. Many have left such misery, though, that their dreams are extremely modest. They want a chance to work hard and make money. The newcomers seem almost eager to endure any adversity in pursuit of their new American ideals.

In one southern state, an entrepreneurial Middle Eastern gentleman established one business—a 24-hour a day truck stop. Needing three shifts of workers, he sponsored friends and relatives from "back home." For their first year, they lived in squalid conditions. After that he bought them a house. Then, another business and another. All employees are Middle Eastern friends and relatives!

Church World Service, a New York-based organization in the forefront of refugee relocation programs, conducted a major survey that showed how refugees are adjusting to their new life in the United States. The study found that within a reasonable period of time they are finding jobs, learning English, and becoming self-sufficient. They added, "And it is *sponsorship programs* that are making these successes possible."[6]

SPONSORSHIP: THE OPPORTUNITY

To leave their home has been a decision few refugees have made easily or voluntarily. Most have left behind virtually everything that is important to them: family, friends, lands, possessions, livelihoods. While some may have had time to gather family members and a few prized possessions, for others there was little or no time to prepare when the bombs started falling or the troops began marching in.

When refugees arrive in their country of resettlement, whether the United States or one of several other countries of first asylum, they are excited by the new life about to begin. At the same time, they arrive exhausted, drained physically, mentally—even spiritually—by their ordeals and losses. Particularly those who have fled war-torn areas arrive with few physical possessions; most arrive with diminished emotional and physical reserves of energy to cope with their new challenges and adjustments.

Sponsorship of refugees involves commitment and responsibilities, but it also has great benefits. Sponsoring individuals and congregations are enriched not only by their contribution to healing a broken world, but also by the new friendships they have made, and with their broadening view of the world. And, ultimately, the possibility of bringing another family into the Kingdom of God!

WHAT IS INVOLVED IN REFUGEE SPONSORSHIP?

The work of the sponsors consists of three essential responsibilities. The first responsibility is that of *enabler*, assisting the refugee with initial material needs and helping the refugee achieve economic self-sufficiency.

The second is that of *friend*, providing the crucial emotional support and guidance needed by the refugee to meet the challenges of overcoming great personal losses and making the major adjustments to his new society.

The third is that of *advocate*, insuring just and decent treatment for the newcomer in this society—without discrimination against other groups—and promoting respect for the cultural heritage and identity of the refugee.

- The enablement responsibility involves:
- Meeting and welcoming the refugees upon arrival at the airport, providing temporary accommodations, as necessary, and assisting in obtaining initial housing and essential furnishings;
- Assuring that food or a food allowance is provided and that the other basic needs of the refugees are met;
- Providing minimum clothing for refugees upon arrival, if necessary;
- Assisting refugees in applying for their Social Security cards and in registering their children for school;
- Providing general orientation to the new community and society;

- Assisting in learning English and enrollment in English as a Second Language (ESL) courses;
- Encouraging and assisting the refugees as soon as possible after arrival to seek public or private health services available locally and assisting refugees with known health problems to secure follow-up treatment as necessary;
- Providing job counseling and assistance in placing employable refugees in a job as quickly as possible;
- Advising the refugees on the availability, advisability and procedure for applying for various training programs.

In most cases, the major responsibilities of the enabling role are carried out within the first three to six months after arrival. Possibly you sense the entire task of enabling is too great for you alone. These responsibilities can easily be shared among people in your congregation in whose hearts God is putting a love for the refugee.

The responsibility of friend involves:

- Offering friendship and providing emotional support to the refugees;
- Offering on-going orientation and appropriate assistance with adjustment problems and concerns;
- Assisting refugees to maintain and share essential elements of their own cultural heritage;
- Introducing them to your Friend, who sticks closer than a brother.

The third responsibility of sponsors as that of advocate includes:

- Insuring that the refugees are not taken advantage of, discriminated against, or exploited in their workplace or personal lives;
- Encouraging contact, communication and bonds with other refugees and mutual support groups

of different backgrounds in our society, including minority groups.[7]

HOW LONG WILL IT TAKE?

When an individual or church decides to sponsor a refugee or refugee family, there is always that anxious question of "How long will I have to wait for my refugee family?" Experience, over the years, has shown that it usually takes longer than people expect. Rough estimates of arrival dates in terms of weeks or months for various refugee groups can be given, but a church should be prepared for a longer wait.

Bringing refugees from around the world first involves identifying legitimate refugee status. Then health clearances and complicated travel plans and delays almost invariably result. Refugee work, without a doubt, demands the development of one of the Christian virtues: *patience!*

WHAT NEXT?

Individuals and churches who will accept the challenge of ministering to these internationals who live among us, and will commit to sponsorship, should contact a refugee resettlement office. An individual or church cannot sponsor except through such an agency:

- Alliance for African Assistance; www.alliance-for-africa.org
- Jewish Family Center; www.jfssd.org/site/Page Server?pagename=programs_refugee_main
- Lutheran Immigration & Refugee Services; http://lirs.org/
- Migration & Refugee Services, U.S. Catholic Conference; http://old.usccb.org/mrs/
- Refugee Resettlement, Church World Service; www.cwsglobal.org/what-we-do/refugees/us-programs/refugee-resettlement.html

- Tucson Refugee Ministry; www.tucsonrefugee ministry.com/
- World Relief; http://worldrelief.org/page.asp x?pid=2054, http://worldrelief.org/page.aspx ?pid=997
- http://refugeehighway.net/regions/north-america

RELOCATED BHUTANESE REFUGEES KILLING THEMSELVES

However, it must be emphasized that working with relocating refugees is not for the faint-hearted. Issues that relocating refugees face do not end once they are settled into a safe community. Most are unable to communicate in English with the host community. Many are still plagued by worries about family back home and the difficulty of maintaining cultural and religious traditions. The push to find employment has many working at tasks far below their skill level. While few had previous mental health problems, the trauma of their path to this new home has many struggling emotionally.

A recent study discovered a high rate of suicide among Bhutanese refugees settled in the United States—a rate almost double that of the general U.S. population. Looking for causes, they discovered the rate of depression among the Bhutanese in America was over three times the general population. Further, suicide runs through the cultural narrative of the Bhutanese. It is a frequent theme in their movies. Those who commit suicide are even viewed as being courageous. Suicide is an open option to dysfunction in Bhutanese culture.[8]

Is the answer to allow them to languish in a distant resettlement camp? There isn't a Christian who would say "yes" to that question. Then, what is the answer?

Here is one answer:

A native of Eritrea, Jirom moved to the United States in 2008 to be with his fiancée, whose family had left the isolated African country several years prior. Like most of the 60,000 refugees who arrived in the U.S. that year, he had little money and few relationships to land on his feet. But a Christian couple, inspired by their church's sponsorship of a large Burmese family, decided to open their home. They gave Jirom a room and one of their cars, helped him and his fiancée navigate marriage paperwork, and enrolled him in a local GED program. And then they employed him: Jirom now works full-time at the Westchester Commons Chick-fil-A, where Spanish, Nepali, Burmese, Tigrinya, and Amharic are spoken to a suburban clientele ordering fried chicken nuggets and waffle fries.

The fast food restaurant of a thousand lands is the work of Erik Devriendt, the owner/operator of this Chick-fil-A since June 2011. Since moving to Richmond in 2006, Devriendt has wielded his vocational skills to address the needs of Richmond's refugee population: namely, steady and life-giving employment. Including Jirom, Devriendt has employed some 20 refugees for his 67-employee team, often receiving referrals from Commonwealth Catholic Charities, the local resettlement agency. The agency helps with paperwork and training, but Devriendt's incentive for hiring refugees is not financial. He simply wanted to "help them in the most tangible way possible, so we stepped up to the plate and took a swing."

Devriendt first learned about the plight of refugees through the Richmond Christian Leadership Institute (www.rcliweb.org), a year-long leadership program that trains Christians to understand the history and cultural dynamics of their city. "I remember hearing from a pastor whose congregation was made almost entirely of refugees from various African nations," says Devriendt, who was part of RCLI's 2007–2008 inaugural class. "I was humbled that the stranger and alien talked about in the Bible were literally in my neighborhood and I didn't even know it."[9]

PEOPLE LIVE THEIR LIVES IN STORIES

Another answer: At last week's prayer meeting, a worship song we sang prompted me to tell a story. I asked, "May I tell a story?" That was certainly "out of character" for me and probably for that assembly. But the song so inspired my memory, I just blurted out my request. They let me tell my story and thanked me for sharing. One brother said, "That really ministered to me." They were drawn into my life by my story. That is what stories can do.

People live their lives in stories. We don't live in outlines or main points or rough drafts. Though the story may change in detail each time it is told (through new memory triggers or a desire to embellish the story), it is a person reliving an important moment or hour in his life.

Immigrants come to our nation with stories. They had a life and a career that they lived before coming to the United States. They need to talk about those lives, which still mean so much to them. Entering their stories allows you to begin seeing the world through the eyes of their culture. A Native American adage said it this way, "To understand a man, you have to walk a mile in his moccasins."

Develop a venue to allow them to tell their story:

- As you and the people in your church relate with the internationals in your neighborhood, workplace, marketplace or at the park, listen to their stories. Ask them if they would like their story told. Establish a sharing night in a community building.
- Help them write their story down. Have someone edit and publish it in a public or Christian newspaper column or a blog.
- Begin your roving, "Meet the Internationals Living Among Us" one-minute video on YouTube. Get your camera going as they tell a snippet of their story. Of course, you will stay to listen to the whole story. And develop a friendship. And possibly even introduce them to *your* Friend!
- There are scores of other ideas that will come out of your imagination as God gives you His creative thoughts.

FROM REFUGEE TO REFUGEE CAREGIVER

Still another answer:

David Schupack, Director of Bridge Builders Network interviewed Walter Lam, founder and director of Alliance for African Assistance (AAA).

David Schupack: You were born in Uganda. Tell us about your journey to San Diego.

Walter Lam: Yes, Uganda was my home. I accepted Jesus as my Lord and Savior in college. I married after graduation from college, immediately after the death of my mother who was my very dear friend. I wanted to get married to Evelyn right away. We had two children, Benad and Julius. I was working in Uganda and everything was going well until a change in government. I was forced to leave my country in fear of my life.

I left by myself. My family came two years later. We initially stayed in neighboring Kenya, hoping and praying that the situation at home would get better. It didn't so we went to Europe, still hoping to return to Uganda. Unfortunately, I did not see any improvement for us to return, so we came to the USA.

DS: People being forced to leave their own nation...that doesn't make sense to us here in America.

Walter: When you are faced with death, decisions to leave come more easily.

DS: But, why San Diego?

Walter: Being granted asylum was a difficult process. We came originally through New York City. I had to apply to the Immigration Office and submit papers to the State Department. The advisor's opinion was that the situation in Uganda had improved, so I was initially denied asylum. But my case was strongly supported by Amnesty International and congressional leaders who wrote favorable letters. Also, we were adopted by friends at La Jolla Presbyterian Church (LJPC), here in San Diego. They have supported us each step of the way, even to the establishing of the *Alliance for African Assistance (AAA)*. They continue to support the organization until today.

DS: By helping a refugee family, the church has multiplied its involvement with refugees. How did the Alliance get its start?

Walter: My first years in San Diego saw me working as a security guard, a dishwasher and a school bus driver. From that foundation, I began to recognize the needs of other refugees here. Seeing them sleeping on the floor and lacking knowledge of where to get help, I asked members of the church for donations of mattresses. They kept donating as I kept showing them the needs of refugees. The church then decided that they needed a refugee resettlement committee within the church. The committee was involved in resettling refugees from Poland and Ethiopia at that time. Churches today cannot directly resettle refugees but they can go through resettlement agencies such as the AAA.

LJPC assigned a deacon to work with me to help set up the Alliance. The church gave $7000 as seed money to start AAA. Our annual budget now is about $4 million. So their gifts and help to me and my family have been multiplied more than a thousand times.

DS: What can a local church do that resettlement agencies such as AAA cannot do?

Walter: Our program is only able to assist for the first 90 days after their arrival. We ask for the help of churches and volunteers to assist with their long-term issues. Their spiritual need, of course, is the most critical need! Who better than volunteers from the churches can meet their hunger for the Lord?

DS: Today, through social networks, Americans are inundated with needs—causes of every sort—needs around the world. Why is helping relocating refugees important?

Walter: Mission committees in most churches are still looking to go overseas—China, Africa. Yes, it is okay to still go overseas to do mission work, but as I see it, *the mission field has been moved right to the doorstep of the churches in America* (emphasis added). Just look around. You don't have to board a plane in order to meet people from Burma or Ethiopia or Uganda. They are right here. So the mission field has completely changed. Unless there are ministries that only can be done over there, right now these people are around us. We need to focus on the people whom God has brought to our own doorstep.

DS: Are churches doing this?

Walter: AAA has quite a number of churches, which are working with us. Also, we are working with other organizations. But as we know from the Bible, the harvest is plentiful and the laborers are few, even right here in San Diego.

We speak at churches educating them to their ability and privilege to get involved in this ministry of resettling refugees. But if a church just one time would meet a refugee family at the airport when they arrive, neither they nor the family will ever forget it. I have never forgotten all the people who helped us through the many challenging times we experienced.

You also learn a lot and grow culturally and spiritually when helping these people. They definitely have different accents and expectations. They have to make adjustments living here. The best way for them to make those adjustments is for people who love God to be there to hold their hand, showing them that "this is the way we do it here." The bottom line is we were all created to worship God. Yes, there are differences between peoples, but these differences can be overcome if we are committed to learn from these people and are able to share what we have. It takes a willingness to learn as well as to impart knowledge.

Looking back on my journey for a moment: Personally in leaving Uganda, going to Europe and then to San

Diego, I never lost my hope. Something that worked very well for me was that my faith kept me alive through all the challenging times. I always knew that I was not alone, but that God was with me during all my struggles. Another constant that helped me through: There was not one single stop point that God did not have His children there to help me and support me—all the way to San Diego. Even today, I have that support. It is so important for all these refugees here, going through challenges, to believe and know and experience that God has His children at every single point of their journeys. Churches and their members may be the children that God has placed here to support the refugees. And the only way anyone can know that is to come out and see. How powerful it would be for each of these refugees to be able to tell a story the same as mine—that at every point in their journey, God's people were there to help.

DS: For me, it was necessary to accept the uncomfortable feelings that came with my initial contacts with people of different cultures. Others may experience some fear or may feel unqualified.

Walter: Who is unqualified to be a friend? In Italy...I still remember this guy...his name was Joseph. An African American guy in the Navy in Pisa, Italy. He had come from Georgia. He became a dear friend. He took me to his church every Sunday afternoon. Who can't be a friend?

DS: Walter, you mention how you always had hope in God in your journey as a refugee. What about those refugees who are coming who have no hope in God?

Walter: Those are the very people that faith based organizations and churches should be rallying around— to support them and give them hope and help them to know God.

I am not resting on my laurels. With the support of my family and church and many other people, I have given the rest of my life to this work. Until God tells me, "I am done with you," this is what I will be doing.[10]

And three more answers:

Bridge Builders Network San Diego has discovered a great need for bridges to be built between Muslims and Christians. They are taking the initiative to facilitate opportunities for positive interaction between the peoples of these two communities. One step they are taking:

> San Diego receives more refugees from overseas than almost every other city in the USA—thousands every year. In the month of August 2012 alone, about 400 [Ed. now 4000] refugees arrived to San Diego to seek a new life. According to Walter Lam, the founder of Alliance for African Assistance, about 60% of the refugees that arrive in San Diego are Muslims. They leave behind them their country where war, poverty, and suffering are the everyday norm. They leave behind family members, their homes and lands, their dreams, and all of their possessions except for two suitcases each. Imagine being in that position just because of your religious convictions, or political beliefs, or because you were born into a certain tribe or clan. Many refugees in San Diego come from what are called "closed nations" where Americans are not welcome, including Afghanistan, Iraq, Iran, and Somalia.
>
> Finding a job is the number one challenge and need for newly arriving refugee families. Many take the most menial of jobs because of discrimination, lack of English language skills, or lack of understanding our culture. Bridge Builders

Network is looking for local Christian business owners and trades-people who are willing to hire newly arriving refugees and see it as a mission that can change the world, one family at a time. If you know of any trades-people or business owners who would consider being a part of a pilot program to hire and mentor refugees, seeing it as a God-honoring ministry opportunity, please contact me for more information.[11,12,13]

JUST ONE MORE STORY

You may be saying, "I never realized there was such an opportunity, but I need one more *nudge* to get started!" Then let me tell just one more story: I met a vivacious and enthusiastic woman, Cherie Gray, giving a seminar in San Diego a few months ago. Listen to how she got started:

I was a teacher for blind students for 9 years and I felt the Lord was telling me to prepare for the mission field. So I packed up everything in St. Louis and moved back home to Tucson, Arizona where my parents lived. I stored my house full of things on their back porch and throughout their home and waited for God to show where He wanted me to go.

While I was seeking the Lord and doing odd jobs, I met a refugee from Bosnia and started teaching her English. Every time I came back to teach her, there were more people from more countries, and I realized they were all refugees who wanted to learn English. So we officially launched an English class in an elementary school nearby, and got several volunteers on board. Meanwhile, I spent most of my free time visiting these new international friends. I would often hear them say

"You're my only American friend." For me, that translated to "You're the only one representing Jesus to me," and it made me wonder—Where is the Church?

Then I had an opportunity to live in the Middle East for a couple of years. I jumped at the chance because I had come to love my Middle Eastern friends so much through the English classes. I got a firsthand education about their culture, their language and their religion. While I was there, God showed me how I could be a bridge between two cultures, and I began to imagine ways that the American Church could be more intentional about embracing our international neighbors back home in the States. I wrote a letter to my pastor detailing how we could do that, and I began praying that God would raise up a team of people who would work together and invite the Church to minister to refugees. Five leaders from five different churches started meeting together even before I came home, praying for God to mobilize churches for international ministry at home. In January 2006, just a few days after I arrived home, we all met together and launched Tucson Refugee Ministry.

We recognized that most churches across Tucson did not have any idea about the international opportunities that were right here in our city. Even though Tucson was resettling nearly 1000 new refugees every year, most Christians didn't even know that they existed. There were two things I focused on as we attempted to connect with refugees, and to educate and mobilize churches. First, I contacted the four resettlement agencies here and jumped through all the hoops to become a volunteer with each one of them. That is the only way they would give me access to meet a refugee. Then I started knocking on the doors of churches that were located in refugee neighborhoods, and asking if I could come and give a presentation about refugees. A lot of doors were opened. Some also remained shut. But after time, each church that got involved told another church because their members were transformed and were beginning to catch a vision for the nations who were at our doorstep. Before long, churches were contacting me to come and speak.

Since then it's been a matter of connecting the dots...matching one church group together with one refugee family. We learned as we went what worked and what didn't.[14]

Working with relocating refugees can be a tremendously rewarding ministry. The variety of activities is as diverse as your abilities. Prayerfully consider this as a ministry to internationals who live among us. Or, consider with me the opportunities with those whom we will meet in the next chapter.

8 ETHNIC COMMUNITIES

A WHITE COLLAR COUNTY NO LONGER

Lon Allison, Executive Director of the Billy Graham Center at Wheaton College, tells this story:

> In DuPage County, Illinois, where Wheaton College is located, we are called a "white collar" county. In 1980, 1 in 14 persons was ethnic non-Caucasian. Today we are 1 in 3. By 2020 we will be 1 in 2.
>
> In our suburban neighborhood of some 50 homes, there are people from many cultures. When a family from India moved into our neighborhood, my wife and daughter delivered homemade bread to welcome them. I like them. Their Christmas decorations are some of the best in our neighborhood. Being somewhat of a Christmas decoration devotee, I can appreciate such attention to Christmas decor. However, I noticed there was no nativity scene in their decorations. Next week we will invite them to our home. The redemptive journey with them will begin. Yes, ethnic persons are coming from everywhere to America. Some bring Christ and we need to empower them. Most do not and we need creative and loving ways to reach them.[1]

The United States is now one of the most ethnically diverse countries in the world. Even in the tragedy of 9/11, 80 different nations were represented among the

3000 who died. Forty per cent of our nation's people are of an ethnic minority. That represents 130,000,000 people who were created by God to worship Him. Twelve million immigrants come to America every year, yet less than 10% are ever befriended by an American, much less by a follower of Christ.

And they just keep coming! Most come legally, many illegally. Several of the groups come and go, others stay. One large group that remains entered legally but is now violating an expired visa. Difficult to locate and deport, they easily elude a faulty system. And invariably those who stay, whether legally or illegally, migrate to *ethnic communities.*

And they just keep coming! The amalgamation of previous generations—thousands of internationals "melting into the pot" of American culture—is not happening today. Fearful, not only of whatever defines "America," but fearful of other ethnic groups, the internationals who live among us are isolating themselves in ethnic communities. Their community becomes a place where they can enjoy the familiar and be protected from those "others"—a place where they are "at home."

The fear and suspicion may show itself in mere isolation: "We have nothing to do with the Mexicans here," sneers Columbian Arturo Price, living in California. "Our culture is different. Our Spanish is more pure." Or cultural bigotry can show itself in devastating riots, where not only racial animosity between two communities flares, but then other ethnic communities enter the fray, venting their rage. And the children, still caught between cultures, form the gangs that perpetuate the separation.

And they just keep coming! In our cities, cultures ten years ago too few to number now register in the tens of thousands. By the 2010 census, Latinos constituted 16 percent of the U.S. population, making them the largest minority group in the country. In 2000, it was estimated that by 2010, they would represent 11 per cent of the US population. The increase is almost 48% greater than projected! Of the 55 million speakers of other languages in the homes of America, 34 million speak Spanish. It is estimated that by 2035, there will be no ethnic majority in the United States; the majority of Americans will be minorities![2]

According to a Pew Research Center study, Asian Americans are the highest-income, best-educated, and fastest-growing racial group in the U.S. They are more satisfied than the general public with their lives, finances, and the direction of the country, and they place more value than other Americans on marriage, parenthood, hard work, and career success. 74% of Asian American adults were born abroad; of these, half speak English very well. The total Asian American population (foreign and U.S. born) was a record 18.2 million in 2011, or 5.8% of the total U.S. population vs. less than 1% in 1965. Non-Hispanic whites are 197.5 million (63.3%), Hispanics 52.0 million (16.7%), and non-Hispanic blacks 38.3 million (12.3%). 430,000 Asians, or 36% of all new immigrants, arrived in the U.S. in 2010, according to the latest census data. That compares to 370,000, or 31%, who were Hispanic. As recently as 2007, about 390,000 of new immigrants to the U.S. were Asian vs. 540,000 Hispanics.[3]

And they just keep coming! And mosques and temples and synagogues enable them to worship as their parents did. The number of mosques and mosque participants continue to show significant growth. The US Mosque Survey 2011 counted a total of 2106 mosques; as compared to the year 2000 when 1209 mosques were counted—representing a 74% increase. Muslims who attended Eid Prayer (the high holiday prayers after Ramadan and Haiji) increased from about 2 million in 2000 to about 2.6 million in 2011. The total Muslim population cannot be accurately determined by this figure, but a safe estimate is a total of up to 7 million Muslims in America.[4]

And they just keep coming! As more and more refugee/immigrants are assimilated into U.S. culture, a new dilemma develops: How to reach and hold the second and third generation "American ethnics." In this simple reversal of words, there is significant difference: Ethnic Americans verses American Ethnics. Ethnic Americans are the first generation immigrants. Though they may have been here for years, they may speak English, or maybe not. They face the challenge to "stay alive" in a strange land where it is difficult to even communicate. They have left "home," their way of life, their work, and their community. Though some may encourage their children to quickly assimilate, others may demand adherence to "the way we always have done it." It is doubtful that they understand cultural nuances or clichés. Their first and primary language is not English. And if you ask them, "Where are you from?" you'll hear "Havana" or "Nicaragua" or "Phnom Penh." They still look to their ancestral country as being "home." After their children are established, some may even return to the "old country."

American ethnics of the first generation, however, find themselves between two worlds: In the school, workplace or community, they have to assimilate, at least on the surface. Dress styles, language, greetings, places to go, things to do will make them appear to have assimilated. Below the surface are the feelings and attitudes, which are being taught by the ethnic American parents, and other relatives who might even live in the same house with them. They will speak the parents' native language at home. The degree of ethnic identity varies with cultures, but as our country is boasting of its new pluralistic freedom, this cultural identity is holding back the American ethnics from assimilating—of "melting into the pot."

A homey illustration was given: Take three ingredients: Delicious brown chocolate chips, rich, white cream and pure, white sugar. When you mix them together in your double boiler, the chocolate chips, the cream and sugar lose their identity to make a delicious candy bar. We are not enjoying the sweetness of candy today in a pluralistic society where most are maintaining their ethnic identity.

While waiting at a lab for my annual blood test, two foreign-speaking ladies sat down next to me. I listened closely, trying to determine which Asian language they were speaking. When there was a break in their conversation, I interrupted: "I have been listening to your conversation, trying to determine your homeland." I had just been in Vietnam, Cambodia and Myanmar. It didn't sound like any of those. I have spent a lot of time in China. No, it wasn't Chinese. It must be Japanese or Korean. "I think you are from Korea," I spoke without much confidence. A big smile came on her face. "Actually, I came here when I was three months old. My mother... (and she gestured to the lady next to her)...and father are from Korea." Notice that she said her parents *are from Korea*. Even though she was born there, in her mind, she was American. Though they have been here for more than 25 years, her Mom does not speak any English, so only Korean is spoken in the home. Yet, the daughter's English was perfect—without accent. In fact, since her college graduation, her job is tutoring internationals in English! My name was called so we did not get further in our discussion, but she was there with her mother to interpret for her. For sure her mother's social interaction would have to be ethnic American, i.e., Korean!

American ethnics, however, of the second- and third-generation have a different orientation. They may be Polish, but their home is Chicago; or Mexican, but their home is Seattle. They are likely to speak (or at least understand) the language of their parents, but their primary language is English. They understand the unspoken cultural connotations of the United States. An American ethnic "gets" an American joke, an ethnic American usually doesn't. An ethnic American would not have been comfortable in an open conversation with me; the daughter, an American ethnic, was.

Most American ethnics are not losing their heritage altogether. They are still aware of their bicultural status. However, they are less and less able to identify with cultural events or patterns, which no longer exist for them or for their parents.

I had an interesting experience with a young lady, Kate, who lived next door to us. Her parents had won the Bulgarian lottery, the method used to determine who of the thousands who apply, are allowed entrance to America. She and her sister had lived here long enough to be American ethnic and U.S. college graduates. It is interesting, though, that they were able to represent Bulgaria at the Athens Olympics and lost to the American team!

Mom and Dad were managers of a senior citizens complex, so seldom came "home." Kate was responsible for the upkeep of their house. One day, shortly after a Southern California fire had destroyed several hundred homes, Kate and I were in the front yard talking about the upkeep of houses and property. In a feeble attempt to turn our conversation to spiritual matters, I said, "Well, some day it is all going to burn," our Christian-speak for "the end of the world!" Her response: "Yes, those fires could have come this way." My indirect communication certainly didn't communicate what I had intended!

And they still just keep coming! If the American ethnic/ethnic American phenomenon were not challenging enough, all that has been described and is yet to be considered is cause of further perplexing entanglement. The holding on to cultural distinctives, the demanding of one's "right" to remain ethnic instead of melting into the pot, has caused deep stirrings in many who had never considered their ethnic heritage. People are reclaiming their past.

In this new caldron, feelings of nationalism—*not* American nationalism—are easily acquired; initially (possibly) for no other reason than novelty or pride. (I do remember my parents' national heritages and I wanted to name my nationality here, but my strong Americanism would not permit it!) Then as loyalties are learned and developed, the ultimate extension is bigotry and hatred, creating neo-Nazis in the North and the revival of the Klu Klux Klan in the South! Yes, there are still private clinics in southern states which have a separate entrance and waiting room for African-American patients!

Further, this circumstance has emboldened certain other recognized minority ethnic communities to rise up and demand recognition of their rights. Thus, we had Native Americans picketing the Atlantic Braves for their "tomahawk chop!" The controversy continues with this and other First Nation-related names and mascots, not only in professional teams but also all the way down to elementary and high school level.

Add to this the simple generational dissonance of an Anglo-American congregation. I was invited to Minnesota to speak at a church about missions. Dress attire for a Sunday morning speaker varies from church to church and state to state, so I asked what would be appropriate for me to wear. I was told to bring a dress shirt, tie and sport jacket, *and* a sports shirt! Interesting. For the first service, I wore the dress shirt, tie and sports jacket. It would have been even more appropriate had I worn a suit. The organ and piano played the old hymns of the church. Second service: Take off the tie and jacket! Just the piano. *Some* contemporary music. Third service: Sport shirt. Piano and organ are rolled off the stage. A band is set up. And we rocked!

Again, I sat on a panel with the Missions Pastor of an African-American church. After the discussion she said she was impressed by a number of my answers. We had not met before, but she invited me to do a seminar at her church. She asked me to sit on the platform on the Sunday before the seminar and be introduced. There was a good turnout for the first Saturday session, but before the second one, she called and said she needed to cancel with the words, "Our people are as prejudiced as your people!"

Years ago Anthony Campolo told of his family's reason for staying in a community that was being overrun by an ethnic community other than "their own kind of people, if you know what I mean." His father had purchased the offering plates for their church. The family name was engraved on the bottom of those satin lined plates. And they were not going to leave those behind!

Into this disjointed, unharmonious, incongruous arena marches the Church of Jesus Christ singing, "We are one in the Spirit, we are one in the Lord...!" And some churches seem to have facilitated a bond of unity—the blend of cultures into the Body of Christ. Others have allowed their facilities to be used at various times by indigenous groups who have developed their own unique koinonia. Still others are training nationals as leaders in separate, but related-to-the-mother-church congregations.

The Krikorian Movie Theater was donated to Shadow Mountain Community Church, a community of believers in El Cajon, California. They converted the theater into their International Ministry Center, which houses many international fellowships, each with their own pastor, ESL classes, their Border Ministry and other cultural outreaches. As I talked with Missions Pastor Dr Gary Coombs, on the phone, I could not keep up with him telling me all the exciting things that are happening through that Center! Because I was recently in Myanmar, one thing did catch my attention. He shared, "On Sunday 110 Karenni people from Myanmar, now living in San Diego are in one of the services. The message is given in Burmese, but it has to be translated for them. They do not speak Burmese or English, nor do they have the Bible in their language. But here they are, living among us!"[5]

One Chinese-American, American-Chinese church in San Diego has three lead pastors. At 9:15, in two different auditoriums are Mandarin and English worship services. At 10:45, in those same two auditoriums are the Cantonese and English worship services. The older generations choose the mother tongue service, which splits up the families. This is possibly okay in American culture, but definitely not in Chinese culture. Another local Chinese church has only English services, except the prayer meeting which is listed on their website in Chinese characters! (Interesting! The American ethnic Chinese don't pray?)

Whether the Church has taken the initiative on these attempts at harmony or if awareness and action has been forced on Her is a moot issue: *Ethnic ministry is upon us!*

However, while this shift is positive, denominational or nondenominational kingdom building and cultural imperialism practiced in other countries for centuries has sadly found its way into "world missions at home." Representatives of the majority culture, especially when they control the funds, often make the mistake of forcing their wills on other people.

I add that there are exceptions overseas and at home. Remember the good model of Mick Ewing in the chapter on International Visitors: *They knew Mick had pastored a church named Calvary Fellowship. They wanted to please him by naming their churches after his. He emphatically said, "There is no way we are going to call the churches there, 'Fellowship of the Skull'!*

A church taking the initiative is great, but individuals can also initiate relationships. Mike relates this story:

> One young engineering student had nearly straight "A" grades at a local State University. He took "Rick" as his American name. He and his siblings choose new names just to avoid classmates making fun of them while they were in school. The cost of doing this brought questioning from his relatives and ethnic neighbors who asked, "Are you ashamed that you come from Vietnam?" As a child, he could not answer them, but later he responded, "I am proud to be Vietnamese, and I am proud to be American. I am in America now." He had been born in Vietnam but came to the U.S. at two years old. His family was part of the evacuations of those who had worked closely with the U.S. military in the war. The family moved into a neighborhood dominated by Vietnamese who shared similar experiences. Although they now speak some English, they mostly speak Vietnamese at home and in the neighborhood.
>
> With outstanding grades in school, a local engineering firm quickly hired him. He did excellent work, but was stagnated at an entry-level position. One of his co-workers, Stan, saw the problem. He decided to befriend Rick and set a plan to help him. Stan told him he had to develop confidence in speaking before groups in order to get promoted. He invited Rick to lunches, Toastmasters meetings, and home fellowship studies. Each venue gave him opportunities to

talk before a group of friendly people who didn't make fun of his accent, as his schoolmates had. Rick saw results—he got his first promotion! His co-workers saw his greater confidence and readily accepted him into company social events. Stan kept working with him, and along the way, answered a lot of questions about the differences between Buddhism and Christianity. Eventually, Rick entrusted his life to Christ.

Now, several promotions later, Rick is a leader of a Christian workplace ministry and is active in telling the Vietnamese-American community, in which he still lives, about Christ. He serves in his church, which has an outreach program to the Vietnamese community. The program has services in Vietnamese and social events that include members from multiple ethnic churches. Rick has gone on several short-term mission trips to Vietnam. He has also translated a number of Christian publications and discipleship materials into Vietnamese. He has been instrumental in leading his extended family to Christ. "That," Rick says, "is my highest accomplishment in life."[6]

It was reported in the *Christian Post* by Alex Murashko that Pastor Derwin L. Gray of Transformation Church in Indian Land, South Carolina, is one of a growing number of Christian leaders in America who want to see churches do a better job of teaching discipleship in order to develop multi-ethnic congregations. The former NFL linebacker said that a key to helping Christians mature within churches that are struggling is to model after the ethnically diverse churches of the First Century.

"As a pastor of an intentional, Gospel-centered, multi-ethnic church, the biggest problem is getting our people to believe that the Gospel of Grace is really as wonderful as it is," Gray told the *Christian Post* via email. "Because we are ethnically, socially, economically, and generationally diverse, we are constantly teaching our people that at the heart of the Gospel is servanthood."

He believes Christians should ask, "How can we embrace one another and learn from one another just like the ethnically diverse churches of the First Century?" Adding, "Unity in the midst of diversity is simply breathtaking and a powerful witness to the unbelieving world."[7]

David Boyd, a New Zealander, started a church in Cabramatta in Sydney, Australia, perhaps the most multicultural region in the world. The church has become a dynamic multicultural church of 500 made up of more than 82 different ethnic groups. Boyd says missions should primarily be a function of the local church, not mission structures. When churches are multicultural, the Gospel can cross cultural barriers within the activities of the church. People become comfortable in this bicultural environment. This prepares them to take the Gospel back to their ethnic groups in their homeland. This is how the Great Commission can best be carried out.[8]

Our model is in the church in Antioch of Syria. Following the downfall of Jerusalem, the Jews were dispersed *"...as far as Phoenicia, Cyprus, and Antioch, preaching the Word to no one but to the Jews only"* (Acts 11:19). They found other Jews and a mono-cultural fellowship was born. However, when some men came from Cyprus and Cyrene to Antioch, *"they spoke to the Grecians, preaching the Lord Jesus"* (Acts 11:20). As the church developed, the ethnic diversity was evident even in the leadership. For, in determining to send out their first missionaries, they put forward five men for consideration who were each from a different ethnic background!

Out of this multi-cultural church came multi-cultural missionaries. Barnabas, though a Jewish Levite, had been raised in the Hellenistic/Roman culture of Cyprus. Paul of Tarsus, though he considered all his past as "refuse for Christ's sake," had the educational advantage of speaking several languages and cultural understanding of more than just Jewish life. And where did this first missionary team go? Back to Cyprus, Barnabas' home culture. A White Paper, *Profile of a Sending Church*, is available at ERI's, ACTS Media Library.[9]

Despite the few bright spots, denominational and non-denominational agencies are eager to plant their "flag" in different ethnic communities, making sure their "label" is clearly visible. A curious footnote to this insensitive, prideful attitude: It was my privilege to attend a fellowship meeting at a denominational church in California, left unnamed to protect the guilty, where the pastor and elder of the newly formed church in Mongolia were speaking.

Now, mind you, this was the first known Christian church in the entire history of Mongolia! (Centuries ago Kubla Khan had asked Marco Polo for missionaries to come. One began the journey to that ancient land but became ill and returned to Europe.) A question and answer time followed their testimony and challenges. I kid you not! The very first question was, "Have you named your church ____?" In the blank, of course, the questioner had put the name of his denomination.

The elder, who had had a lot of contact with Americans, as he was a guide to American wild game hunters in Mongolia, wisely answered, "We have named our church the First Presbyterian, Southern Baptist, Methodist, Assembly of God, Brethren Church of Mongolia." When laughter broke out—letting him know they had gotten his point, he said, "No...you know, we have just named it the Bible Church of Mongolia!"

Whereupon, the pastor of this American church quickly interjected that they were in the process of training and sending a worker of *our* denomination to Mongolia and, pointing to the Mongolian pastor and elder said, "We will be glad to have you work with her when she arrives!"

Unfortunately, few have taken the full compass of culture and language seriously enough in the training of their workers or in demonstrating a willingness to allow ethnic churches to develop without cultural and denominational restrictions imposed by the larger organization.

We must come to terms with the reality of a multi-cultural society. Acquisition of a second language is increasingly more important for Christian workers. We must be trained in cross-cultural adaptation. We must be equipped with new kinds of materials—ones that aren't just English language materials translated into Laotian. That won't work for the ethnic American. Now we need materials written by Laotian Americans for Laotian Americans, by Hispanic Americans for Hispanic Americans. It will take that kind of understanding of bicultural patterns to reach today's ethnic Americans *and* American ethnics. It will take an enormous commitment. It can be done. Will *you* be a part of it?

Excellent resources are available to help educate you and people in your fellowship who are joining you in this exciting venture of faith: Cross-cultural ministry in your neighborhood, your church, your workplace, and your marketplaces.

Brian Virtue at brianvirtue.org would be a good place to start. Two well-articulated articles give us perspective on various attitudes toward ethnic minority ministry, one from the majority culture and the other from the minority culture.[10,11] Another good source of help comes from an organization called The Coaching Center. They have an excellent piece on understanding ethnic communities.[12] Loving Our Religious Neighbors (LORN) Campaigns encourage us to produce fruit of the Spirit in a multi-religious culture.[13] A "thousand" other resources are just a click away on Google: "Ethnic communities." You certainly want to be intentional about your involvement. Listen to Sarah's story in her pursuit to be intentional in cross-cultural ministry in New York:

Hi, my name is Sarah and I am twenty-two years old. Four and a half years ago I moved to New York to go to NYU and study theater. When I was a sophomore, one Sunday I was reading Isaiah 58. I was challenged by the way I was living my life. I went to church and worshipped in all the right ways but I wasn't spending myself on feeding the hungry or meeting the needs of the oppressed. So I started spending my free time eating with the homeless people around NYU while every night returning to my Fifth Avenue downtown apartment. Something began to feel out of place.

Around that time I began to read the Gospel of Matthew with my friend Jillian. We asked ourselves, 'What if we took the words of Jesus seriously, and didn't water them down?' We decided the answer to that for us was to move just 15 miles away to South Bronx, the poorest neighborhood in the United States.

The Bronx has the highest rate of poverty in the U.S. More than half the kids that live there live below the poverty line, two out of every three adults are unemployed, sixty percent of the people don't have a high school diploma and only four percent of the people in my neighborhood have graduated from college. Needless to say, drugs, crime, gangs and prostitution are rampant. Violence is a normal part of survival.

Our biggest obstacle at the beginning was that everyone, from the cops to our Christian community thought we were crazy. The cops told us that our neighborhood was a war zone and that we had to get out. I remember sitting on my stoop one night and watching the families walk by. I thought to myself, 'Who's fearing for the safety of these kids. As long as they are forced to walk home on these streets...I will too.'

As we began to focus on being present in the neighborhood, we realized that the people we were supposed to be afraid of greeted us by name and gave us big hugs every time we walked by. Before long, kids were hanging out at our house until midnight and asking for food. We realized that no one was taking care of them. Most of them were living with one guardian who was either strung out on drugs or working three jobs. So we started giving them after school snacks and helping them with their homework, feeding them their dinner and putting them to bed in their homes every night.

All of this was happening while I had a full time job that I not only loved but found myself with a huge amount of power and influence and wealth within the company. However, I was working more and more hours each week and had less and less time to read Bible stories to the kids or be there for my neighbor when she was diagnosed with AIDS. I had to make a choice.

So, after wrestling for months, I quit my job and decided to raise support to give all of my time, energy and creativity to being a part of God's renewal in my neighborhood. I don't know where the money is going to come from but I have faith because I know that I am in the center of God's Kingdom becoming a reality on earth. The poorest neighborhood in America is in the most powerful city in the world.

As a part of Grace Trinity Church, I am committed to see God's Kingdom come in New York, which to me means people from Chelsea and the Upper East and West Sides coming alongside our brothers and sisters in the South Bronx, living together, worshipping together and breaking bread together. As the people of God we're called to steward our privilege on behalf of the poor in our city. What an honor that God uses our small acts of obedience to bring His Kingdom into forgotten neighborhoods. This is just the beginning of God's work in the South Bronx of New York City.[14]

Are you ready for such a radical commitment? From Sarah's small beginning—a true incarnational image of Christ—has come a strong ministry in the South Bronx. As you read further about *A House on Beekam*, you will appreciate the joyful commitment these people have made to see a transformation in the lives of individuals and in the whole community.[15]

TRANSFORMATION

The desired end result is seeing transformation take place in individuals and neighborhoods. Transformation is a permanent change in one's attitude, belief, and behavior in all areas of an individual's life (physical, spiritual, emotional, social) that then facilitates the same changes in others; who then as a group change their neighborhood from the inside out.

An Approach that Fosters Transformation
- It requires a moral and ethical focus for relationships to grow, which results from establishing trust.
- These ethical values are based on absolutes that do not change, but are the same year-after-year. They are based on God's Word, the Bible.
- It is a people-oriented, relationship building process.
- It is designed to identify assets within the neighborhood (found in individuals, associations and institutions), and identifies which of those assets they are willing to share.
- Once the assets are identified, people are linked around their common interests.
- The desire is to see people begin to take responsibility for their own lives and then as a group for the life of their neighborhood.
- It is based on neighbors helping neighbors, not being dependent on professionals to dothings for them.
- It is designed to build up internal and external abilities.
- It is designed to be sustainable.
- It is primarily a grass-root, bottom-up process that requires a person to act as a catalyst and facilitator.
- It is a gradual learning process, progressing from the simple to the more complex and from the known to the unknown.
- It works primarily with individuals and households and then impacts the neighborhood as a whole.
- It is greater than the sum of its parts.[16]

If you find Sarah's bold move too radical for you at this time, listen to Harold's story:

My wife an I are involved in work that takes us out of the city too often to get deeply involved in local church ministry. For a while we were satisfied to remain "lost" in a big church. Nobody knew when we were there or when we were gone or when we came back!

One day as we were thinking about this, we realized we could be supportive of a small church just by faithfully being there when we were in town. Where? was our question. We had heard about a large church that had moved out of a deteriorating inner city area into the suburbs. "Was there a Gospel message left there?" we wondered.

Yes! A small band of people was going from civic buildings to rented church facilities to afternoon services in a park, just to keep a Light in a very dark area. From the sounds of it, it is where Jesus would have hung out: prostitutes, homosexuals, drug addicts, attempted suicide victims and all the physical ailments that accompany such people and activity. A few members arrive on powered wheel chairs. Several carry their oxygen tanks. One lady brings her puppy dog. Several walk with a cane. Recovering drug addicts can look quite fierce until the love of Jesus softens them.

We have found our place among them. They welcomed us in to become part of the family. Cultural diversity? Yes, but as we got to know the people, color and physical features and language differences disappeared. I initially struggled with the Mexican men kissing my wife during the greeting time, but that got worked out. The ethnic Mexican pastor one Sunday called the glory of God, Chicano instead of Shekinah! But we are all there to worship the one true God. It's a bit of a drive from our house, but being a part of a multi-ethnic, multi-cultural community is worth it.

Cities probably will remain the focal point of the ethnic mix. But the suburbs increasingly will feel the impact of foreign cultures, and suburban churches will be forced to respond. Will they view the change as a "foreign invasion" or will more Christian attitudes prevail? Will the churches take the lead in demonstrating acceptance of ethnic people and appreciation for their language and culture?

God questioned Jonah, *"Should I not be concerned about that great city?"* (Jonah 4:11) He was speaking of Nineveh, the capital of ancient Assyria, located on the northern shores of the Tigris River. It was a city with an estimated population of 1,000,000 (*"...120,000 who were not old enough to make moral judgments"*). And today, the movement of populations from the countryside to cities has created more than 50 cities in the USA with a million or more souls. If we listen carefully, echoing down through the corridors of time, we will hear our God saying, should I not have compassion on such great cities. Whether your city is a large megalopolis or a small country village, it is likely the internationals living among you have made efforts to congregate into ethnic communities.

Take a look at Chicago!

IMMIGRANT CHICAGO

Steve Franklin said that Chicago is the world. But don't take his word for it:

> Explore the city and you will discover restaurants, social services, museums, and houses of worship that bind Chicago to places across the globe.

You may think you are tuning in on a short-wave radio if you visit some neighborhoods flourishing with newly arrived immigrants. Chicago's public schools count over 100 foreign languages spoken by their students, with Spanish leading the pack by a wide margin.

What makes Chicago different? In most major U.S. cities there are one or two immigrant corridors. In Chicago there are three major corridors with branches reaching out from them, along with a number of smaller communities reflecting other nationalities.

The heart of Latino Chicago is found in the Pilsen and Little Village neighborhoods on the city's Southwest Side. But smaller Latino neighborhoods sprawl across the city and region. Altogether Latinos account for nearly 30 percent of Chicago's residents, with a total of over 1.8 million Latinos in Chicago and its suburbs. Mexicans make up the bulk of the area's Latino population, followed by Central Americans and smaller numbers of South Americans.

On Chicago's Northwest Side and spiraling north and south is the Eastern European corridor. Poles account for the vast majority of this community. It is said with pride that Chicago is second only to Warsaw in the size of its Polish population. But there are also significant numbers of Serbs, Romanians, Lithuanians, Russians, Bulgarians, Slovenians, and Croats in that sector. Visit the third corridor, Devon Avenue on Chicago's North Side, and you will discover a bustling commercial street that stitches together a rapidly growing Indian, Pakistani and South Asian community. As is true for other immigrant communities, Devon Avenue has become the anchor—a place to shop and dine—while many immigrants are leapfrogging the city to plant their roots in nearby suburbs.

Narrowing your focus you will find a thriving Chinatown just below Chicago's Loop and a second, newer Chinatown on Chicago's North Side that includes a mixture of Vietnamese, Thai and other Asian communities. Similarly, you will find Arab communities on the North and South Sides of the city. Lately African immigrants have begun to stake out their own place on Chicago's North Side, but pockets exist on the South Side as well.[17]

ETHNOBURBS

Beyond this, now enter the ethnoburbs! It is such a new term that it is not yet in my computer dictionary. Ethnoburbs—suburban ethnic clusters of residential areas and business districts in large metropolitan areas—are multiracial, multiethnic, multicultural, multilingual, and often multinational communities in which one ethnic minority group has a significant concentration but does not necessarily constitute a majority. An ethnoburb functions as a social hub and a place where immigrants may work and do business within their own cultural network. These communities are often more directly connected to the global economy and world politics. Further, they bring distance from urban crime and racial "others."[18]

Dr. Wei Li, who coined the term, came to live in Monterey Park, California, to work on her doctoral thesis on the suburban Chinese population of Los Angeles. She identified that area as a suburban Chinatown. But as she continued her research, she discovered it to be much more than that. With over 60,000 people, it joins eight Asian dominated ethnoburbs stretching through 25 miles of the San Gabriel Valley.

Studies of these new urban communities show that the ghettos of yesteryear are slowly disappearing. The Little Italys, Chinatowns, Germantowns and other ethnic enclaves of poor, struggling immigrants are giving way to this new neighborhood—the ethnoburb. It is no longer found in the inner city slums. Its broad, tree-lined streets look like any middle-class American suburb. Its uniqueness, though, rests in the makeup of the ethnoburb. In that San Gabriel Valley, for example, you could visit the Great Mall of China. A play on words, for sure, but you will find it crowded with Chinese restaurants, authentic Chinese teashops and high-fashion stores. This San Gabriel Square, its formal name, is located in the middle of a prosperous suburb with a majority-Chinese population. You could spend a day walking around the stores and shops and hear nothing but Mandarin or Cantonese.

German ethnoburbs have transformed Milwaukee, Wisconsin and Cincinnati, Ohio. Italians have clustered in communities in Philadelphia and Baltimore; Irish in Boston and Butte, Montana. The fastest growing region (2013), however, is Riverside County, California. Latinos dominate the population with 45.5 percent, the largest ethnic group, dwarfing the Anglos [European descent] as a minority with 36 percent of the population. But for all the ethnic growth from the south, the Asian influx to America's new demographics dominates the scene. Without a doubt, internationals are living among us. Or, possibly, we are living among them! It is projected that by 2021, Caucasians will be a minority in America.[19]

A MANMADE TRAGEDY

As I introduce this final "ethnic community," I hang my head in shame. As I did the research, I felt like I should not even call myself an American. Rather, an international who is living among the Americans. I am speaking, of course, about the First Nation Americans, more rudely referred to as Indians. I read about the history of Native Americans and Christianity and the atrocities of Christian leaders against those American nationals who didn't convert.[20a] I read about various denominations who have tried to reach across extreme cultural barriers to communicate the love of Christ, yet with little success.[20b] I read interviews that clarified the "problems"—such as the fact that suicide is the second leading cause of death among Native American youth. Suicide rates for 10-14 year olds is four times higher that for all U.S. races.[20c] I read about the hopelessness in living conditions where there is no indoor plumbing or electricity...that they live on wasteland where rainfall is less than the evaporation rate.[20d] Article after article speaks about the "problem."

This *Religion Today* article best summarizes the challenges:

> Picture in your mind's eye the souls of thousands facing a Christless eternity. The situation is desperate. Laborers in this harvest come before the Lord burdened with heavy hearts, having witnessed...emptiness, yearning, anger, escape, drunkenness, overdose, jail time, divorce, revenge, and heartache. The vicious cycle of a life without Christ is merely a slow suicide. Does anyone care?" ask Scott and Kathy Murphy of the Regeneration Reservation in Fort Thomas, Ariz.
>
> Thankfully, yes. Many do care. A number of Christian organizations devote their time and resources to serving Native Americans in North and South America. AmeriTribes, American Indian Bible Ministries, Native Harvest, Warriors for Christ and Flagstaff Mission to the Navajo are just a few of the Christian organizations reaching out to tribal people.

There are 2.5 million American Indians and some 550 different tribes in the United States alone, says Huron Claus, president of Christian Hope Indian Eskimo Fellowship (CHIEF) ministries. The Canadian government reports another 800,000 First Nation, indigenous people within its borders.

Reaching native people presents a series of challenges. "First, in the eyes of many, Christianity has been seen as the white man's religion," says Claus, himself a Native American. "As a result, we've had the gospel for 500 years, yet less than 8 percent of our Native people are believers in the Lord."

According to NNM, the Native Ministry division of the Southern Baptist North American Mission Board, many tribal members interpret Christian evangelistic efforts to mean they must give up the heritage that is so sacred to them. In other words, most tribal people believe they have to stop being Native American in order to be a Christian. Because of this misconception, the gospel message is often met with a cold reception.

The most effective means of sharing the gospel in a Native American context, is for Native American believers who have come to trust Jesus as their personal Savior to tell people in their own tribal context how Jesus has made a difference in their lives.[21]

Where is the solution? I believe it is found in that last paragraph: *The most effective means of sharing the gospel in a Native American context, is for Native American believers who have come to trust Jesus as their personal Savior to tell people in their own tribal context how Jesus has made a difference in their lives.*

And that is exactly what Randy and Edith Woodley are doing. Randy is a recognized legal descendent of the United Keetoowah Band of Cherokee Indians in Oklahoma. Edith is a member of the Eastern Band of Shoshone Indians. Their four children are Leanna, Skye, Young and Redbird. Together, the Woodleys use their gifts to minister God's love to people. They are forerunners in the current move of God, in what is today called the Native American Contextual Movement.

Randy Woodley, PhD., founded Eagle's Wings Ministry as a community of Native Americans and others, rooted in the Christian faith. He states, "We work, through word and deed, to reach Native Americans and others with the good news of Jesus Christ, while respecting native cultures, and with concern for individual and social transformation.

"Based on the native 'harmony way' tradition of spiritual health, family, social, and environmental balance, our purpose is to promote the prosperity and well-being of Native American communities in ways that are culturally contextual, holistic in scope, and based in community.

"Central to fulfilling our purpose is a commitment to leadership training appropriate to traditional indigenous cultures."[22]

In sober contemplation of what you have just read, I trust you can bow your knee in humility and pray to God about what He would have you do. What *can* you do? It is best expressed in the commitment Bruce and Linda Farrant made:

> There are over 1100 Native American/ First Nations people groups on the North American continent (excluding Mexico). After 500 years it is estimated that only 2-5% of these indigenous people profess to be believers

in Christ. Historically, our government and its representatives have consistently broken treaties and trust with Indigenous Nations. Many atrocities and injustices have been endured, often committed in the name of "Christianity." Why should they now consider the "religion" of these that have not kept their word? Walls of anger, hurt, and mistrust must be broken down and replaced with trust and acceptance to make way for reconciliation and the message of hope. This takes time; this takes humility. We must be willing to listen, to learn—something we failed to do in the past. It is a two-way street, for we need them speaking into our lives.

Reconciliation is long overdue. It is time to reach out to build relationships, to "love our neighbors." Life among Native peoples is first of all relational, and relationships take time. There must be commitment to friendship for the long haul. We cannot just talk about the love of God, it must be demonstrated, "fleshed out" and tangible.

How does the vision become reality? For churches and people who have a desire to become involved in building relationships with Native American/First Nations peoples, here is a possible path:

Commit to praying for Native Nations across the U.S., Canada, and Alaska.

- Focus prayer on a specific Tribe or Band, learning all you can about them.
- Search your library and the Internet to gain insight and information.
- Host seminars for the purpose of preparation and greater understanding.
- Commit to investing in long-term relationships before ever making contact with any people.

- Pray for an opening for contact.
- Pray for a man, woman, couple, family who will commit their lives to a group of people and be willing and prepared to support and encourage them. This step is high priority!
- Consider the possibilities of sending in teams under Tribal authorities or ministries with established contacts. Only go with a group that gives training before going.
- Develop partnership within churches for this venture.[23]

After reading this chapter, the Holy Spirit may have tapped you for reaching into ethnic communities with the love of Jesus Christ. And there is an abundant supply of resources to further educate you and help you in your involvement.[24]

Possibly the whole subject has been overwhelming. I am overwhelmed by the magnitude of the challenge! But there is not another chapter to read! Since you have read this far, you have shown a definite interest in the internationals who are living among us. If you have not yet sensed with which group the Lord wants you to minister, may I suggest that you accept the challenge that I put forward in the Epilogue that follows, asking the Lord to show you where your gifts and talents would best be used for His glory.

And then, *JUST DO IT!*

EPILOGUE

I am excited and challenged to see that God has brought the internationals of the world to live in ethnoburbs of Chinese and Italians and Latinos and Germans and _____. Name the cluster of ethnics near you. Maybe you are now living in one, as Lon Allison and his family are, in DuPage County, Illinois, who wrote in Chapter Eight.

I am excited and challenged by the multi-ethnic face of America. The 1965 Immigration and Nationality Act has made the United States one of the most ethnically diverse countries in the world, creating additional ways to fulfill the Great Commission. Truly God has brought the nations of the world to the doorstep of every church in America.

I am excited and challenged to look on a picture of the eternal scene playing out in our country: That from *"every tribe, tongue, people and nation"* (Revelation 14:6) there are those worshipping God.

I am excited and challenged to realize that this unity expresses an answer to the Lord's prayer, *"May they be brought to complete unity to let the world know that You sent Me"* (John 17:23).

I am excited and challenged by the open receptivity of many ethnic people to the Gospel. (More ethnic Muslims have trusted in Christ in the past ten years than in the previous 300!)

And I am excited and challenged by the care and caution that must be exercised so that we don't repeat the mistakes in our communities that were made in the past by overseas missions. It will take a fresh out-pouring of spiritual wisdom, faith and most of all humility to work together for God's Kingdom. It can be done. It must be done.

MY FINAL APPEAL

You have followed with me through a mere thumbnail sketch of seven types of internationals who live among us. They came for various reasons and stayed for varying lengths of time. Each brought various hopes and expectations, fears and apprehensions. And each came needing a unique approach for ministry. Yet, they are unified by their one need for Christ. For no matter what search brought them to America, they will find true fulfillment only in a right relationship with God through Jesus Christ.

These internationals who live among us present a new challenge to the church in America. It is an opportunity of gigantic proportion. The "melting-pot" effect of past generations is not true today. Some immigrants, even those who have been here for two or three generations, are maintaining their cultural distinctives. So, with all their unique characteristics, they are here, living among us. At the very doorsteps (sometimes literally) of every church in America.

While this or that group gets caught up in the "flesh and blood" social-ethical-economic-political issues of them being here, let it be said of you, that you did *"not take advantage of* [nor ignore] *aliens in your land; you did not wrong them. Rather, you treated them like any other citizen. You love them as yourself!"* (Leviticus 19:33-34)

So, my final appeal is A Call to Prayer—A Call to Action.

A CALL TO PRAYER

We do not need to pray for the harvest. The harvest

is obvious. The harvest is ripe. The more bizarre the vain pursuits of man become the more we realize how dissatisfied he is with what this world offers.

We do not need to petition God as though He were reluctant to save the lost. He is willing, ready and wants to do that. His eternal heart is beating to the pulse of Peter's words, *"God is not willing that any perish, but that all come to repentance"* (II Peter 3:9).

We do not need to ask Him for physical resources. For all of our "recession/depression," we are the richest nation in the world. Our poverty level is in the top fourteen percent of world wealth. The physical resources are available.

Our call to prayer is singular. Our prayer is patterned after the cry of our compassionate Christ. As He looked over the multitudes, who appeared to Him as sheep without a shepherd, He turned to His disciples and said, *"Pray to the Lord of the Harvest to send forth laborers into His harvest fields"* (Matthew 9:38).

I challenge you to see the multitudes of *Internationals Who Live Among Us* as sheep without a shepherd. And bend your knee at this call to prayer.

Then, on a very curious note, in the very next verse, Jesus says, "Well, men, you did a great job praying! Now for the ACTION! You're it! You are the harvesters I plan to send out!" Not quite KJV English, but... (Matthew 10:1).

A CALL TO ACTION

Ethnocentrism—focusing only on my kind—seeks to divide us. But as followers of Jesus we have a message of peace and hope for our neighbors. We must affirm the fact that God loves all people and that He wants us to love each other.

The late Roberta H. Winter of the US Center for World Missions said: "Like a master chess player, God has moved representatives from unreached people groups far from their homelands all over the world and has plunked them down in the midst of traditionally Christian populations, essentially saying, 'They have come to you. Now tell them about Jesus!'"

Or, as Doctor Luke said it in Acts 17:26-27: *And He (God) has made from one blood every nation [ethnos] of men to settle on the face of the earth, having definitely determined beforehand their allotted periods of time and the fixed boundaries of their dwellings [their settlements, lands and abodes]. His purpose was for the nations [ethnic communities] to seek after God and perhaps feel their way toward Him and find Him—though He is not far from any of us."*

God has placed the internationals of the world in our neighborhoods. The mandate is clear: *Love them as yourself.* The opportunities to express love are as varied as the interests and abilities of the person sitting next to you in church. As Dr. Hiro asked, "How much effort does it take to be a friend?" It begins as simply as that. Let's allow the Lord of the Harvest to send us forth into His fields—the ripe fields of harvest right here in America?

Let's do *world missions* at home!

END NOTES

CHAPTER ONE: INTERNATIONALS AMONG US
1. Excerpted from "Ellis Island" by B. Colin Hamblin: http://sydaby.eget.net/swe/ellis_island.htm
2. View the Golden Eagle Award-winning documentary, *Island of Hope – Island of Tears*: http://archive.org/details/gov.ntis.ava15996 vnb1
3. Pew Hispanic Center: http://www.pewhispanic.org
4. El Norte: http://www.imdb.com/title/tt008548 2/
5. World Refugee Day: http://www.abc.net.au/unleashed/2764446.html
6. http://www.ndphr.net/2013/04/refugees-flee-fighting-in-shan-state.html

CHAPTER TWO: BUILDING BRIDGES TO INTERNATIONAL STUDENTS
1. Excerpted from *International Students*, a publication of ISI: www.isionline.org
2. Excerpted from *World Vision*, a publication of World Vision International: www.wvi.org
3. ISI; http://en.wikipedia.org/wiki/Yōsuke_Matsuoka
4. Excerpts from various website on international students: http://www.ifiusa.org;
5. http://www.acmi-net.net; http://www.reaching campus.com

6. Perspective on the World Christian Movement: www.perspectives.org
7. Bronson & Evelyn Stilwell; used by permission
8. Excerpted from Dr. T.V. Varughese article on International Students, www.idminc.org
9. Matt Smucker, ISI: www.isionline.org
10. More good ideas:
    a. http://unreachednewyork.blogspot. com/2012/12/the-greatest-missions-opportunity-in-us.html
    b. http://www.catalystservices.org/wp-content/uploads/2012/06/International-Students.pdf
    c. http://missionscatalyst. net/?p=3019#more-3019
    d. http://www.dualreach.org/missions/ bm%7Edoc/tool-package-college-care.pdf
    e. http://www.prismpgh.org/
    f. http://clearingcustoms.net/2012/10/16/ too-many-international-students-in-the-us-have-no-close-american-friends/
    g. http://www.ifiusa.org/
11. Cheryl Converse-Rath, Tutor/Mentor
12. Wichit Maneevone: http://wichitandmiriam maneevone.weebly.com

CHAPTER THREE: MISSIONARY KIDS: CITIZENS OF THE WORLD

1. Excerpted from *Cascades of Youthful Thought,* Yarinachoca School, 1972
2. "Susan" is a composite of a number of students with whom the author has related
3. Joyce Reed, www.OnlineCollege.org
4. Six Myths: Excerpted from an article: "Toward a Greater Understanding of the Real MK" by Larry W. Sharp

5. A Heart Made Willing, an Mp3 download from ACTS Media Library, www.eri.org
6. *Prepare For Battle! Basic Training in Spiritual Warfare* was written out of our missionary experiences: www.eri.org
7. Generous excerpts from various website and articles throughout the Action Steps section
   a. http://www.dualreach.org/missions/bm%7Edoc/GI_0606.pdf
   b. http://www.mislinks.org/practicing/missionary-kids/
8. "An MK Declaration," Beth Knight, WHEREVER MAGAZINE, Spring 1985
9. *The Reentry Team*: www.eri.org
10. Some useful resources
    a. http://www.iched.org
    b. http://www.mukappa.org/
    c. http://www.upwithmks.com
    d. http://gatehouseministries.org
    e. http://www.brigada.org/today/articles/mk_resources.pdf
    f. http://michelephoenix.com/mk-tck-resources/

Chapter Four: Illegal Aliens
1. A five-hour DVD, *For Those Who* Go: http://www.eri.org/index.php?option=com_content&view=article&id=50&Itemid=39
2. http://www.huffingtonpost.com/2012/08/15/alexander-wang-lawsuit-dismissed_n_1778059.html
3. A Google search provides more statistics than we can comprehend. Throughout this chapter, any reference to statistics has come from Google.
4. http://www.highbeam.com
5. http://www.safe-families.org

6. U.S. State Department
7. FBI
8. U.S. Department of Justice
9. U.S. Immigration and Customs Enforcement
10. http://www.ucpress.edu/book. php?isbn=9780520268661
11. http://www.desiringgod.org/blog/authors/ ben-reaoch
12. Some useful resources
    a. http://www.healthconsumer.org
    b. http://www.freemedicine.com
    c. http://www.immigrantsandiego.org/about
    d. http://www.christianpost.com/news/illegal-immigration-our-national-shame-45892/
    e. http://livingsenttoday.blogspot. com/2013/06/intersection-of-faith-politics-what.html

CHAPTER FIVE: INTERNATIONAL VISITORS
1. *The Guest Room Hospitality Handbook*, Christian Life Workshops
2. Read *The Emmaus Road Story*: www.eri.org
3. John Townsend: www.mt25v34.com
4. Excerpted from *Mission: America Harvesting At Home* by Denny Gunderson
5. Personal interview with Anne
6. Some useful resources
    a. _____ *(city, state of interest)* Visitor Information Center
    b. Accessible _____ *(city of interest)*
    c. http://www.ifiusa.org

CHAPTER SIX: INTERNATIONAL BUSINESS PEOPLE
1. Adapted from: www.martialeagle.net/military leades.html
2. Adapted from: www.namma.org/

3. Dianne works here each summer: www.facebook.com/bsmission
4. Adapted from *Diverse Cultures* by Kathie Hinnen in The San Diego Union
5. http://www.ccesco.com/idm/htm/abouttv.html
6. Current contact: http://soar-rd.shinshu-u. ac.jp/profile/en.OFANuUyU.html
7. http://www.martialeagle.net

Chapter Seven: Relocating Refugees
1. Adapted from issues of *WORLD VISION* Magazine: www.WorldVision.org
2. Calvary Chapel, East Anaheim, CA; Costa Rica Mission
3. A Google search of "Tamil Refugees" will give you the latest information
4. http://www.unhcr.org/pages/49c3646c125. html
5. Adapted from *WORLD VISION* Magazine: www.WorldVision.org
6. Church World Services: www.wcsglobal.org
7. Adapted from *WORLD VISION* Magazine: www.WorldVision.org
8. The Atlantic; April 13, 2013
9. http://www.christianitytoday.com/ thisisourcity/
10. www.alliance-for-africa.org
11. www.Bridgebuildersnetwork.net
12. www.smlouisville.com
13. http://worldrelief.org/page.aspx?pid=2798
14. www.tucsonrefugeeministry.com

Chapter Eight: Ethnic Communities
1. http://www.wheaton.edu/Academics/Faculty/ A/Lon-Allison
2. http://www.migrationinformation.org/Feature/ display.cfm?ID=927

3. http://www.mediapost.com/publications/article/177459/asian-americans-setting-the-bar.html#axzz2VB1A4SMM
4. http://usatoday30.usatoday.com/news/religion/2011-01-27-1Amuslim27_ST_N.htm
5. http://www.shadowmountain.org/default.aspx?page=3390
6. http://www.mt25v34.com
7. http://www.derwinlgray.com
8. http://www.davidmays.org/BN.html/ (Search: You Don't Have to Cross the Ocean to Reach the World)
9. http://www.eri.org/index.php?option=com_content&view=article&id=85&Itemid=62
10. http://www.brianvirtue.org/leadershipdevelopment/five-postures-towards-ethnic-ministry/
11. http://resources.epicmovement.com/sixpostures/
12. http://gocampus.org/modx/index.php?id=197
13. http://www.lorneighbors.com/
14. http://redeemercitytocity.com/join-the-movement.jsp
15. http://www.AHouseonBeekman.org
16. http://www.neighborhoodtransformation.net
17. http://chicagoistheworld.org/
18. http://en.wikipedia.org/wiki/Ethnoburb
19. *Ethnoburb: The New Ethnic Community in Urban America* by Dr Wei Li
20. Resources for First Nation Americans
    a. http://rationalwiki.org/wiki/Native_Americans_and_Christianity
    b. https://www.rca.org/sslpage.aspx?pid=3615
    c. http://www.missionfrontiers.org/issue/article/chief-christian-hope-indian-eskimo-fellowship-training-native-americans-to

    d. http://www.cbn.com/cbnnews/337439.aspx
21. http://www.religiontoday.com/articles/
    missionaries-to-native-americans-face-many-
    challenges-1144000.html
22. http://www.eagleswingsministry.com/
23. http://pcamna.org/church-planting/church-
    planting-ministries/nativeamerican/
24. Other excellent resources
    a. *Reaching the World in Your Own Backyard* by
       Rajendra Pillai
    b. Ethnic America Network;
       http://ethnicamerica.com
    c. http://www.jdpayne.org/2013/05/09/106-
       representatives-of-unengaged-unreached-
       peoples-in-the-united-states/
    d. http://networkedblogs.com/KXWl6
    e.   http://www.nayajeevan.org/resources/
    f. http://gocampus.org/modx/index.
       php?id=197
    g. http://www.globalmissiontraining.com/
    h. http://www.reachingthenationsamongus.
       org/
    i. http://www.cityreaching.com/
    j. http://www.christforallpeoples.org/
    k. http://www.ethnicembraceusa.net
    l. http://www.multilanguage.com/esl/
       LookInsideAmerica.htm